Tapestry Crochet

Written, Illustrated, and Photographed by

Carol Norton

DOS TEJEDORAS

Fiber Arts Publications

Book design by Patrick Redmond

Projects designed by Carol Norton

Edited by Karen Searle

Production assistance provided by Linda Bryan
and Catherine Fleischman

Computer graphs by On-Line Design

Printed by Kaye's Printing, Fargo, North Dakota

Front cover photo: Detail of "Clock Face,"
tapestry crochet project worked in modacrylic carpet yarn.
See page 67.

An instructional video for this book has been produced by
Victorian Video Productions, Colfax, California.

ISBN 0-932394-15-9
Library of Congress No. 91-075151

Published by

DOS TEJEDORAS
Fiber Arts Publications
P. O. Box 14238
Saint Paul, Minnesota 55114

Dedication

I dedicate this book to:

My parents, Elsie and Vincent Woychowski,
who taught me to dream;

My friends, Doris Bush and Nancy Ewart
who helped turn this dream into reality;

And to my husband, Harold, and daughter, Ilsy,
for making many more dreams come true.

Detail, tapestry crochet pillow. Instructions begin on page 59.

Contents

Detail of a tapestry crochet pillow being worked in the round. See project instructions on page 59.

Introduction

Tapestry crochet, also known as "Jacquard" or "Mosaic" crochet, enables the craftsperson or artist to create unique and sturdy clothing accessories, baskets, and intricate tapestries with only a few dollars worth of equipment. It differs from ordinary crochet in its texture, tension, and how colors are worked.

From 1976-1980 I was a Peace Corps Volunteer working with an artisan cooperative in the Guatemalan highlands. While in Guatemala, I bought some colorful tapestry-crocheted shoulder bags. They have held up well under all of the abuse that I have given them, and promise many more useful years of wear.

A tapestry-crocheted shoulder bag is an important part of the Mayan Indian man's traditional outfit. Used for carrying seeds in planting season, and also for carrying lunch or dinner, these bags are not only beautifully crafted, they are also very functional. The shoulder bag is the only item of traditional clothing in Guatemala that is not made by women. Even though many Indian men have turned to western-styled clothing, most continue to make and use their traditional shoulder bags. See *Plate 2*. If a man does not crochet his own, he buys one at the local market, since some men produce extra bags to supplement their meager incomes.

The art of crocheting was probably taught to the colonial Indians by the Spaniards. The Maya have incorporated their own regional color combinations and design motifs. Each region in Guatemala has distinct color combinations and design motifs. Regional stylistic differences in clothing were encouraged in the 1500s by the Spanish rulers, and these still prevail. These differences can be seen in the variety of bags pictured in *Photo 1* (next page) and *Plates 1 and 3*.

Tapestry crochet is not limited to Guatemala. In some areas of Africa and South America, colorful hats are crocheted by local artisans.

After my return to the United States, I became interested in the tapestry crochet technique, and became intrigued with its design possibilities.

The first tapestry crochet piece I made was a Christmas stocking for my daughter. I wanted a strong, large, seamless stocking with an attractive motif. I decided to try the kind of stitch and design used in my Guatemalan shoulder bag. Next, I crocheted the shoulder bags shown in *Photo 2* and *Plate 12,* using my own design motifs. As I worked, I thought about other tapestry crochet projects. The more I thought, the more excited I became as I realized the potential of tapestry crochet.

I developed a method of diagramming the tapestry crochet stitches and design motifs. Eventually, I created a pictorial wall tapestry, modifying the technique so it could be worked flat. Tapestry crochet is usually worked in *rounds,* with only the face of the single crochet stitch showing. When working on a flat piece, turning it over to reverse direction at the end of each row causes the back of the single crochet stitch to show on alternate rows. I wanted just the face side of the stitches to show in each row. After a lot of experimentation, I resolved this design problem. Two flat tapestry projects are included in this book.

As a teacher of crochet classes in a community education program, I found that the main problem both beginning and advanced students had was in trying to interpret the abbreviated directions found in most crochet publications. Students ended up writing out the instructions in long hand in order to follow them. Consequently, I have avoided using abbreviations and asterisks in this book. When a sequence has to be repeated, it is stated in complete words and sentences. Each project is charted, providing detailed visual instructions as well. Along with the forthright directions, clear photographs and illustrations further demystify each project. The general instructions in *Chapters One* and *Two* are written for both right- and left-handed crocheters. *Chapter Three* contains techniques for additional stitches, for adding borders, and for working back and forth.

Chapter Four contains tips on designing your own tapestry crochet piece. A series of projects are found in *Chapters Five, Six* and *Seven*. Each project included in this book covers a different aspect of tapestry crochet, in the number of colors used, its shape, complexity of design motifs, or type of yarn used. Once these variations are mastered, the craftsperson will be able to modify yarn size, design, color, and shape to create original projects. Tapestry crochet may be used successfully to create an unusual gift, or an intricate work of art.

Photo 2. "People" shoulder bags, some of the author's first experiments with designing for tapestry crochet. Left, bag crocheted in modacrylic carpet yarn. Right, bag crocheted in eight cable cotton. A detail appears on page 40. The bags are shown in color in Plate 12.

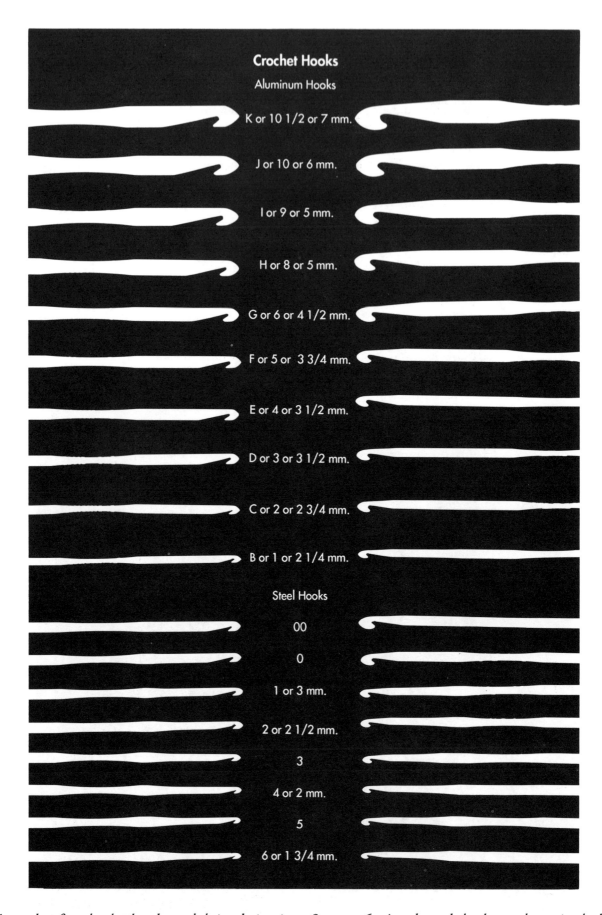

1. *Two styles of crochet hook styles and their relative sizes. See page 6. Angular style hooks are shown in the left column, rounder style hooks are shown in the right column. Hook sizes in both colums range from #6, or 1 3/4 mm, bottom, to #K, or #101/2, or 7 mm. at top.*

I have used a variety of yarns for the projects in this book to demonstrate that many types are suitable for tapestry crochet. The important factor is that the stitch be crocheted *tightly.* Tightness not only hides the carried yarns, but also contributes a stiff quality to the finished piece. Experiment and find the degree of tightness that is right for you.

Other yarns may be substituted in all of the projects. If a thicker yarn is used, the hook should be proportionately larger; if a finer yarn is selected, a smaller hook should be utilized. Stitches may be increased or decreased at the beginning of each project to accommodate the different yarn.

Suitable Yarns and Threads

Photo 3. Some of the yarns used for the projects in this book. Clockwise, from top: five cones of 100% wool carpet yarn, two balls and a skein of heavy crochet cotton, four skeins of acrylic 4-ply yarn, three skeins of acrylic rug yarn, and three cones of modacrylic carpet yarn. Skeins can be wound into a ball using a ball winder.

Commercial yarns are dyed in large batches or lots, each with its own dye lot number. Since dye lots can, and usually do, vary from batch to batch, it is important to purchase extra yarn. If you should run out of yarn before finishing a project, it is unlikely that you will be able to match the color that you need exactly, resulting in a noticeable color variation, or streaking in the piece.

Some yarns will end up stiffer after blocking because of their inherent properties. The 100% polypropylene that I used was the stiffest when blocked, followed by the modacrylic carpet yarns. See *Suppliers List* for yarns used for the projects in this book.

I found that the modacrylic carpet yarns and carpet wools were easier to work with than the acrylic yarns were, because they have more body and split less. String, rope, wire, or any bendable material can be combined with or substituted for yarn to create interesting results.

The graphs included with each project indicate dark, medium and light color shades. I have not indicated specific yarn colors for each project. It should be your choice. Keep in mind that darker colors are harder to work with because they are more difficult to see. I have also omitted mentioning brand names of yarns. Many different companies manufacture the same type or a similar type of yarn. It is up to you to decide what you like best.

Crochet Hooks

Two different types of crochet hooks are manufactured. One style is rounder, and the other more angular. See *figure 1,* page 4. I have found that both styles work well, although each style tends to be slightly different in size. Notice in *figure 1* that the hooks in the right column are slightly larger than the hooks in the left column. Some crocheters prefer one style over the other, but this is a personal preference.

• *Steel hooks* come in small sizes and are usually used with fine crochet cottons.

• *Aluminum hooks* are larger, and usually used with heavier yarns.

A specific hook size is recommended with each project in this book, but you may vary the size of the hook depending on your needs. If you tend to crochet loosely, increase the tension on the yarn or use a smaller hook to crochet a tighter stitch. Sometimes it is necessary to both increase the tension *and* decrease the size of the crochet hook to achieve the desired result.

One major crochet hook manufacturer produces a hook with a larger, easier to hold handle. *(figure 1.1.)* See *Suppliers List.* I highly recommend this new hook. It is much easier to grip, especially when crocheting tightly.

1.1. Wide-handled crochet hook.

Do not be upset if occasionally a crochet hook breaks. I never thought it possible, but I have broken a number of hooks. Sometimes the hooked end will fall off, other times the handle will snap in two.

Use four-ply beige yarn (it's easy on the eyes) and a size D crochet hook to practice the stitches as you read this section. (See *Suppliers List* for materials sources.)

- *If you are left-handed,* follow the instructions for left-handed crochet.
- *If you are right-handed,* follow the instructions for right-handed crochet.

Practice the *slip knot,* the *chain stitch,* the *single crochet stitch* in rounds, inserting the hook, carrying colors, and the *tapestry crochet stitch* until you feel at ease with them before going on to the first project.

Sampler

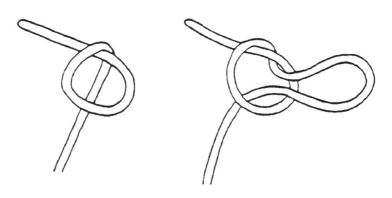

2. First loop for slip knot.

To begin to crochet, make a *slip knot.*

- Begin by making a loop. *(figure 2.)*

- Pull the yarn from behind the loop through the opening to form another loop. Tighten the slip knot by holding the loop to the right while pulling both ends of yarn. *(figure 3.)*

3. Slip knot completed.

Left-Handed Single Crochet

Tensioning

The technique illustrated will allow you to work with the degree of tension necessary for tapestry crochet. To begin:

• Loop the yarn around the little finger of your right hand, then in front of the little, ring, and middle fingers, and then around your index finger a couple of times. *(figure 4L.)*

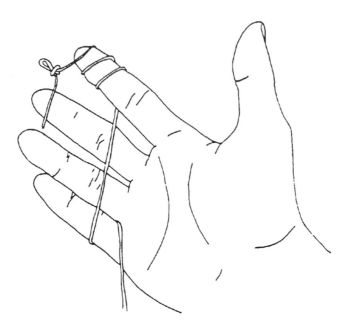

4L. Yarn tensioned around right fingers.

• Grasp the crochet hook with your left hand, resting your thumb and middle fingers on the flat part of the crochet hook. *(figure 5L.)* If you are used to holding your hook a different way, it would be better to change your grip since it is much more difficult to crochet tightly in any other manner.

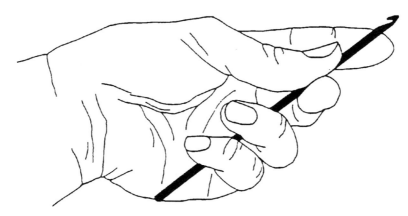

5L. Correct grip on crochet hook.

The technique illustrated will allow you to work with the degree of tension necessary for tapestry crochet. To begin:

• Loop the yarn around the little finger of your left hand, and then in front of the little, ring, and middle fingers, and then around your index finger a couple of times. *(figure 4R.)*

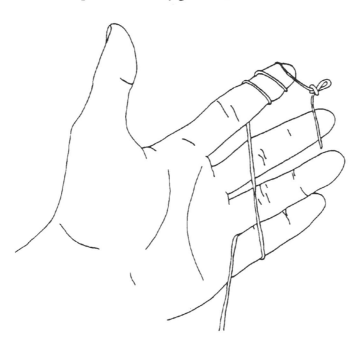

4R. Yarn tensioned around left fingers.

• Grasp the crochet hook with your right hand, resting your thumb and middle fingers on the flat part of the crochet hook. *(figure 5R.)* If you are used to holding your hook in a different way, it would be better to change your grip since it is much more difficult to crochet tightly in any other manner.

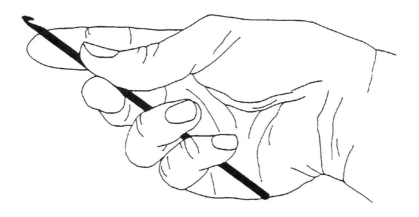

5R. Correct grip on crochet hook.

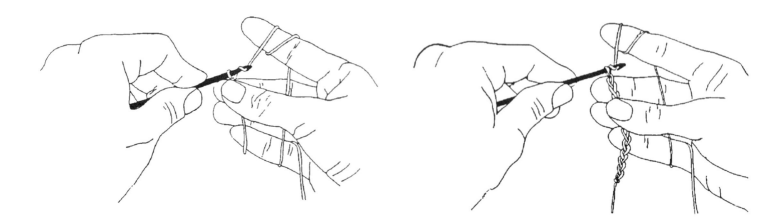

Left-Hand Stitch Technique

To make a chain stitch foundation:

- Hold the slip knot between your thumb and middle fingers. Insert the hook into the loop of the slip knot. *(figure 6L.)*

- Tighten the slip knot around the hook. Flip the yarn over the hook from left to right and then catch it with the crochet hook. This is called yarning over.

- Rotating the hook downward, pull the yarn through the loop of the slip knot. Tighten the new loop on the hook slightly. This makes one chain. Yarn over again, and then pull it through the loop on the hook.

As you use up the yarn, pull up two more inches. You can also unloop the yarn around your index finger as you need it.

To continue the work:

- Hold the chain between the thumb and middle fingers of your right hand. *(figure 7L.)*

- As the chain becomes longer, move it down, creating a slight tension between the chain, hook, and index finger. Insert the hook into the remaining loop, being careful not to split the yarn, and then continue to crochet.

To *rip out* the chain, or any other crochet stitch, remove the hook from the loop, and then pull on the yarn.

6L. (left) Hook inserted in slip knot with yarn over.

7L. (above) Holding the chain.

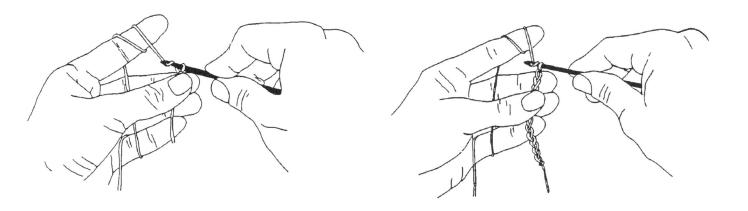

6R. (above) Hook inserted in slip knot and yarn over.

7R. (right) Holding the chain.

To make a chain stitch foundation:

- Hold the slip knot between your thumb and middle fingers. Insert the hook into the loop of the slip knot. (*figure 6R.*)

- Tighten the slip knot around the hook. Flip the yarn over the hook from right to left and then catch it with the crochet hook. This is called yarning over.

- Rotating the hook downward, pull the yarn through the loop of the slip knot. Tighten the new loop on the hook slightly. This makes one chain. Yarn over again, and then pull it through the loop on the hook.

As you use up the yarn, pull up two more inches. You can also unloop the yarn around your index finger as you need it.

To continue the work:

- Hold the chain between the thumb and middle fingers of your left hand. (*figure 7R.*)

- As the chain becomes longer, move it down, creating a slight tension between the chain, hook, and index finger. Insert the hook into the remaining loop, being careful not to split the yarn, and then continue to crochet.

To *rip out* the chain, or any other crochet stitch, remove the hook from the loop, and then pull on the yarn.

Right-Hand Stitch Technique

Left-Handed Single Crochet in Rounds

The Eyeglass Cases, Change Purses, Pillow, and Rectangular Shoulder Bag projects are all worked in the round.

To practice single crocheting in *rounds*.

• Make a slip knot, then chain 12 stitches.

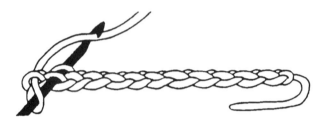

• To start the round, insert the hook from front to back through the bottom loop of the second chain to the right of the hook. Yarn over and then pull it through the chain. (*figure 8L.*)

8L. First stitch being worked into the chain.

• You now have 2 loops on your hook. Yarn over, and then pull it through the 2 loops on the hook. You have just crocheted a left-handed single crochet stitch. (*figure 9.1L.*)

9.1L. Completion of first left-handed stitch.

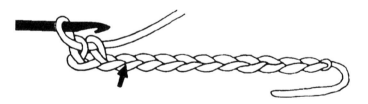

• Single crochet another stitch by inserting the hook where the arrow is, again through the bottom loop. (*figure 9.2L.*)

9.2L Position of next stitch indicated by arrow.

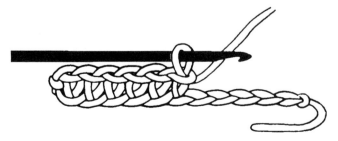

• Continue to single crochet across the row, working from left to right. (*figure 9.3L.*)

9.3L. Left-Handed stitches continued across the work.

The Eyeglass Cases, Change Purses, Pillow, and Rectangular Shoulder Bag projects are all worked in the round.

To practice single crocheting in *rounds*:

• Make a slip knot, then chain 12 stitches.

8R. First stitch being worked into the chain.

• To start the round, insert the hook from front to back through the bottom loop of the second chain to the right of the hook. Yarn over and then pull it through the chain. *(figure 8R.)*

9.1R. Completion of first right-handed stitch.

• You now have 2 loops on your hook. Yarn over, and then pull it through the 2 loops on the hook. You have just crocheted a left-handed single crochet stitch. *(figure 9.1R.)*

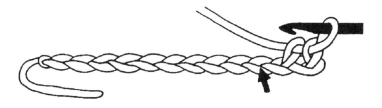

9.2R. Position of next stitch indicated by arrow.

• Single crochet another stitch by inserting the hook where the arrow is, again through the bottom loop. *(figure 9.2R.)*

9.3R. Right-Handed stitches continued across the work.

• Continue to single crochet across the row, working from right to left. *(figure 9.3R.)*

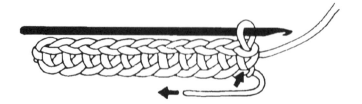

- For the second half of the round, work 2 more stitches into the last chain stitch in the space indicated by the arrow, then pull the short tail of yarn. *(figure 10.1L.)*

10.1L. Turning at end of row.

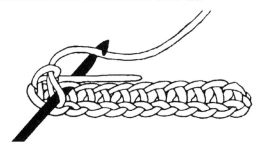

- Turn the piece around so that what was on the top is now on the bottom. Single crochet on the new top through the foundation chain where the arrow indicates. *(figure 10.2L.)* This is a real deviation from traditional crochet.

10.2L. Turned piece.

- Insert the hook through the new top of the foundation chain and under the end piece of yarn. *(figure 10.3L.)* Continue to single crochet as before, crocheting under and over the end piece as you go along.

10.3L. Beginning second half of the stitch.

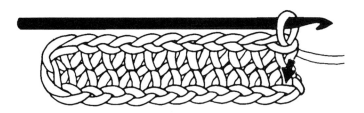

- This completes the first round of single crochet. Insert the hook where the arrow indicates to start the second round. *(figure 10.4L.)*

10.4L. Completed round.

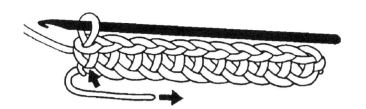

10.1R. Turning at end of row.

• For the second half of the round, work 2 more stitches into the last chain stitch in the space indicated by the arrow, then pull the short tail of yarn. *(figure 10.1R.)*

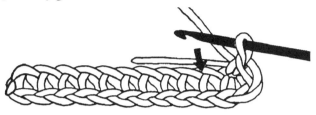

10.2R. Turned piece.

• Turn the piece around so that what was on the top is now on the bottom. Single crochet on the new top through the foundation chain where the arrow indicates. *(figure 10.2R.)* This is a real deviation from traditional crochet.

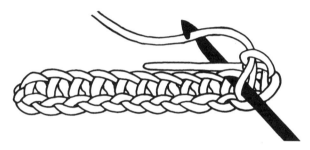

10.3R. Beginning second half of the

• Insert the hook through the new top of the foundation chain and under the end piece of yarn. *(figure 10.3R.)* Continue to single crochet as before, crocheting under and over the end piece as you go along.

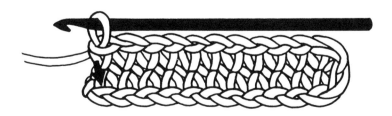

10.4R. Completed round.

• This completes the first round of single crochet. Insert the hook where the arrow indicates to start the second round. *(figure 10.4R.)*

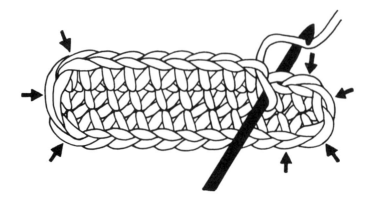

• Continue to single crochet around, inserting the hook now under the two top loops of each stitch of the previous row. *(figure 11L.)* Care must be taken to crochet only one stitch into each end stitch as indicated by the arrows, to create a vertical tube.

Crochet at least five more rounds before going on to *Chapter Two.*

11L. Round almost completed.

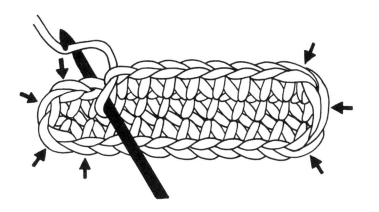

11R. Round almost completed.

- Continue to single crochet around, inserting the hook now under the two top loops of each stitch of the previous row. *(figure 11R.)* Care must be taken to crochet only one stitch into each end stitch as indicated by the arrows, to create a vertical tube.

Crochet at least five more rounds before going on to *Chapter Two*.

Photo 4. Detail of a traditional Guatemalan shoulder bag, author's collection.

2. Tapestry Crochet

The tapestry crochet technique will enable you to crochet a two – or more – color motif with relative ease. While one yarn is being worked, another yarn is carried. At any point the yarns can be switched. The carried yarn is then crocheted while the previously worked yarn is carried. A graph paper design can be used to indicate the color change sequence, stitch by stitch. Special graph papers are provided that duplicate the shape and angle of the crochet stitch.

One important consideration in working with multiple colors is that all of the yarns being worked should be of the same weight to avoid a warped appearance. If a thin yarn is used with a thicker yarn, the thick yarn will occupy more space when worked, warping the piece. I learned this lesson with "Self Portrait." (See *Photo 5* and *back cover*.) Before I was finally able to have it successfully blocked, it had a large bow in the lower portion. A curved perimeter was the final result.

Tapestry Crochet Basics

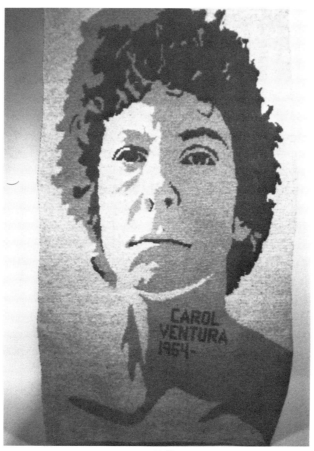

Photo 5. "Self-Portrait," the author's first crocheted wall tapestry, measuring 4' x 7.5'. Note the irregular border. This work is included in the Fiberarts Design Book II (Lark Books). See detail on back cover.

Inserting the Hook
Left Hand

In tapestry crochet, after the first row or round has been crocheted, the hook is always inserted from front to back, under the two top loops of the stitch being crocheted into. *(figure 12L.)* The front of the work will almost always be facing you. The only time it is not facing you is with the *reverse single crochet* technique, page 36.

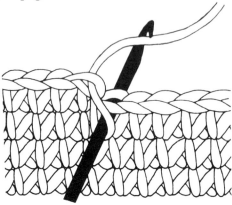

12L. Inserting the hook from front to back.

Carrying Colors
Left Hand

Being able to carry colors is essential for tapestry crochet, allowing a two-or more color design to be worked without floats on the back. The concealed colors make the finished piece more durable. The carrying technique enables knots and loose ends to be eliminated as well.

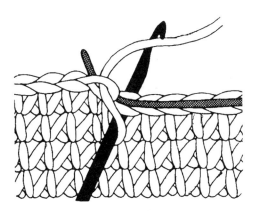

• To carry a yarn, first, lay the additional yarn over the top two loops of the stitches being crocheted into, leaving a one-inch tail sticking out of the back. The carried yarn can be kept in place with the thumb of the right hand. *(figures 13.1L. and 13.2L.)*

13.1L. Second color yarn laid across the top of the work.

In tapestry crochet, after the first row or round has been crocheted, the hook is always inserted from front to back, under the two top loops of the stitch being crocheted into. *(figure 12R.)* The front of the work will almost always be facing you. The only time it is not facing you is with the *reverse single crochet* technique, page 36.

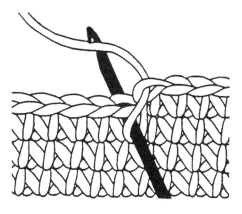

12R. Inserting the hook from front to back.

Being able to carry colors is essential for tapestry crochet, allowing a two-or more color design to be worked without floats on the back. The concealed colors make the finished piece more durable. The carrying technique enables knots and loose ends to be eliminated as well.

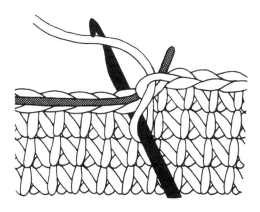

13.1R. Second color yarn laid across the top of the work.

• To carry a yarn, first, lay the additional yarn over the top two loops of the stitches being crocheted into, leaving a one-inch tail sticking out of the back. The carried yarn can be kept in place with the thumb of the left hand. *(figures 13.1R and 13.2R.)*

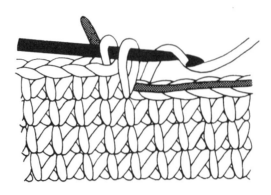

• Single crochet across the row as usual, keeping the carried yarn on top of the loops, crocheting under and over it. *(figure 13.2L.)* If done correctly, the carried yarn will not be visible from either the front or the back of the work.

13.2L. First color worked over the second color.

After the row has been completed, the one inch end (that you left sticking out of the back of the piece) can be snipped off.

More than one color yarn can be carried at the same time for a multicolored tapestry crochet motif. Try to limit the carried yarns to two or three to avoid a tangled mess. Each yarn carried will slightly increase the height of the single crochet stitch. For a consistent appearance, start to carry the yarn at the beginning of a project, even if there will not be any color changes for a few rows.

Joining in
New Yarns
Left hand

If you should run out of the yarn that you are crocheting with, start to carry the new yarn five or more stitches before it is needed, instead of tying on a new piece. Switch to the new yarn, and then carry the tail of the old yarn five or more stitches to secure it before snipping it off.

The carried yarn should be gently tugged occasionally to assure that it does not stick out of the piece where it sometimes becomes slack.

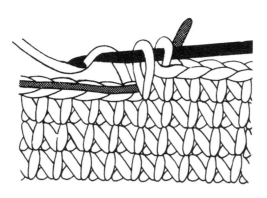

*13.2R. First color
worked over the
second color.*

• Single crochet across the row as usual, keeping the carried yarn on top of the loops, crocheting under and over it. *(figure 13.2R.)* If done correctly, the carried yarn will not be visible from either the front or the back of the work.

After the row has been completed, the one inch end (that you left sticking out of the back of the piece) can be snipped off.

More than one color yarn can be carried at the same time for a multicolored tapestry crochet motif. Try to limit the carried yarns to two or three to avoid a tangled mess. Each yarn carried will slightly increase the height of the single crochet stitch. For a consistent appearance, start to carry the yarn at the beginning of a project, even if there will not be any color changes for a few rows.

If you should run out of the yarn that you are crocheting with, start to carry the new yarn five or more stitches before it is needed, instead of tying on a new piece. Switch to the new yarn, and then carry the tail of the old yarn five or more stitches to secure it before snipping it off.

The carried yarn should be gently tugged occasionally to assure that it does not stick out of the piece where it sometimes becomes slack.

**Joining in
New Yarns
Right Hand**

Left-Handed Tapestry Crochet Stitch

The *tapestry crochet* stitch is similar to the *single crochet* stitch. The difference is that one or more yarns are carried along while the working yarn is being crocheted over them.

To work the *tapestry crochet* stitch:

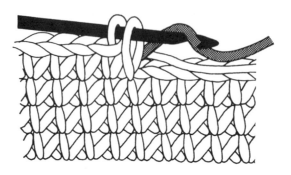

• Switch the yarns while *two* loops of an incomplete single crochet stitch are on the hook. *(figure 14.1L.)*

14.1L. Partial stitch made with first color. Second color picked up.

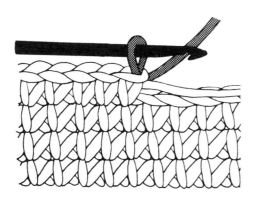

14.2L. Stitch finished with second color.

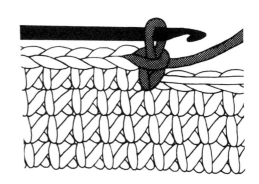

• Make the final yarn over and loop with a *carried* yarn. *(figure 14.2L.)*

• Continue the single crochet stitch across the row while carrying the previously crocheted yarn, until another yarn change is desired. *(figure 14.3L.)*

14.3L. Work continued with second color over first color.

After a few yarn switches are made you will notice that the yarns begin to tangle. Stop and untangle them before it becomes a problem. This is also a good time to check for mistakes.

The *tapestry crochet stitch* is similar to the *single crochet stitch*. The difference is that one or more yarns are carried along while the working yarn is being crocheted over them.

To work the *tapestry crochet* stitch:

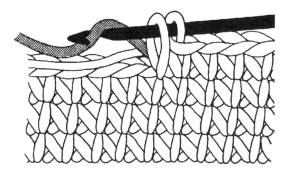

14.1R. Partial stitch made with first color. Second color picked up.

• Switch the yarns while *two* loops of an incomplete single crochet stitch are on the hook. *(figure 14.1R.)*

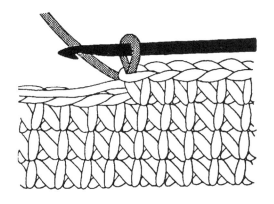

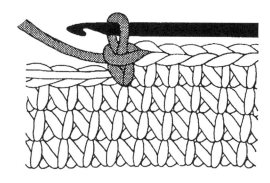

14.2R. Stitch finished stitch with second color.

• Make the final yarn over and loop with a carried yarn. *(figure 14.2R.)*

• Continue the single crochet stitch across the row while carrying the previously crocheted yarn, until another yarn change is desired. *(figure 14.3R.)*

14.3R. Work continued with second color over first color.

After a few yarn switches are made you will notice that the yarns are beginning to tangle. Stop and untangle them before it becomes a problem. This is also a good time to check for mistakes.

Tapestry Crochet Tips

Both Hands

The following techniques are used by both right and left-handed crocheters. Illustrations are for right-handed crocheters. Left-handed crocheters should place a mirror to the side of each illustration to reverse it.

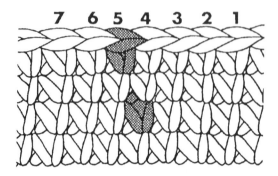

Counting Tapestry Crochet Stitches

The Tapestry Crochet stitch is a *V-shaped* stitch, topped by two loops which also form a V. To count the stitches, either count the Vs in the body of the piece, or count the V loops on top. In the illustration above, there are seven complete stitches across the top, and four rows. *(figure 15.)*

15. Counting stitches.

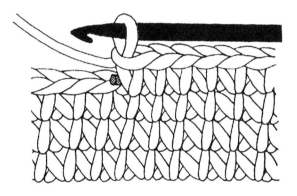

Cutting a Yarn Flush

Cut the desired yarn as close as possible to the finished piece. Cut only those yarns that have been carried for at least five stitches to assure that they are well-anchored. *(figure 16.)*

16. Second color cut flush against the work.

Checking the Gauge

Gauge is important in tapestry crochet. If a piece is crocheted too loosely, the carried yarns will show and the piece will not have a stiff, sturdy appearance.
To check the *stitch gauge:*
• Lay a ruler on top of the project that you are working on. Place the ruler parallel to the rows and line up one of the inch markers between any two stitches. *Photo 6* shows the 5-inch marker lined up correctly.
• Count the number of stitches between the lined up marker and the next inch marker. This will give you the *stitches per inch* measurement.

Photo 6. Measuring stitch gauge.   Photo 7. Measuring row gauge.

In *Photo 6* the measurement is 10.5 stitches per inch since there are 10.5 stitches between the 5 and 6-inch markers.

To check the *row gauge:*
- Lay a ruler on the piece perpendicular to the rows. Line one of the inch markers up between 2 rows. In *Photo 7*, the 5-inch marker is lined up correctly.
- Count the number of rows between the lined-up marker and the next inch marker. This will give you the *rows per inch* measurement.

In *Photo 7* the measurement is nine rows per inch, since there are nine rows between the 5- and 6-inch markers.

Adjusting Tension

If you find that you crochet loosely, use a smaller hook, or crochet with more tension. The yarn wrapped around your index finger controls the tension. Pull the yarn with this finger after each stitch to increase tension.

Shaping Tapestry Crochet

Tapestry crochet can be shaped by increasing or decreasing stitches. Practice the following shaping techniques.

Increasing

To *increase* the number of stitches in a row or round:
- Single crochet two stitches in a spot ordinarily reserved for one stitch. *(figure 17.1.)* Insert the hook back into the same stitch as indicated by the arrow on the left. *(figure 17.2.)*

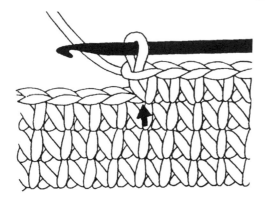 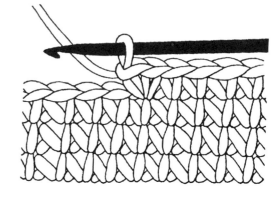

Decreasing

To *decrease* the number of stitches in a row or round:
- Start a normal single crochet stitch by inserting the hook under the two loops of the stitch that you are crocheting into. Yarn over and then pull through a loop. Now instead of completing the single crochet stitch, insert the hook into the next stitch where the arrow indicates. *(figure 18.1.)*

- Yarn over and then pull through a loop. You now have *three* loops on your hook. Yarn over and then pull it through all three loops. *(figure 18 2.)*

- Insert the hook into the next stitch as indicated by the arrow to continue crocheting across the row. *(figure 18.3.)*

17.1. (left) Position of increase stitch.

17.2. (above) Second stitch made.

18.2. (center) Loops pulled up in two consecutive stitches.

18.1. Arrow indicates skipped stitch.

18.3. (below) Decrease completed.

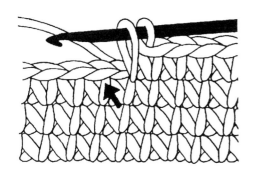 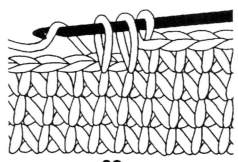 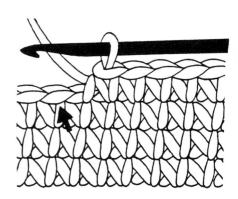

Creative use of increasing and/or decreasing was used to make the variety of projects in this book. If a piece is crocheted without any increases or decreases, it will maintain a constant width or diameter. By increasing or decreasing the stitches on a round or row, the width or diameter can be changed.

To crochet a flat, round disk, *regular increases* expand the diameter. For a proportioned and even look, space the increases and decreases evenly. For instance, if 12 increases are desired in a round of 36 stitches, work an increase into every third stitch.

Cylindrical pieces

When the increasing is stopped, the rounds will maintain a constant number of stitches and vertical walls will emerge around the flat disk, creating a basket shape. If the number of stitches is again increased or decreased, an interesting shape can be achieved. For sculptural or organic-looking pieces, increases or decreases can be placed anywhere as needed. *(figure 19.)*

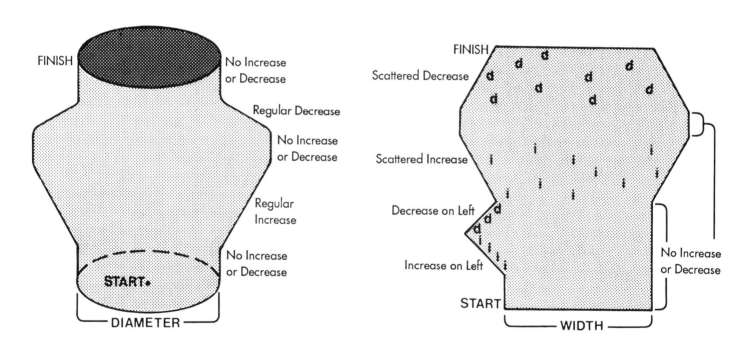

19. (above) Cylin-drical shaping.

20. (right) Flat shaping.

On a flat piece, stitches can be added or subtracted at the beginning or end of a row, or evenly or randomly spaced throughout a row. Each method will create a different look. *(figure 20.)*

Flat Pieces

Frequently the piece will appear warped or lumpy. These minor flaws are easily removed during blocking. A major warp or lump however is usually lessened only slightly through blocking.

Finishing Off
Slip Stitch

Tapestry crochet can be finished off very neatly, and the yarn ends worked into the fabric.

To finish off:

• Insert the hook under the two loops of the stitch being crocheted into as usual. Yarn over, pull through a loop of yarn, and then continue to pull the yarn right through the loop on the hook. This is a *slip stitch.* Cut the yarn, leaving a 6-inch end. *(figure 21.1.)*

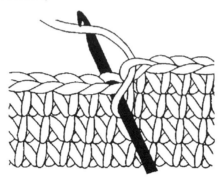

• Yarn over and then pull the 6-inch end completely through the loop on the hook, thereby locking the stitches to prevent any unraveling. *(figures 21.2 and 3.)* The 6-inch end should then be worked into the piece to secure it.

21.1. Yarn over for slip stitch to finish off.

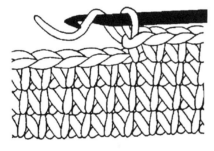 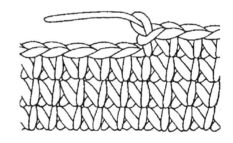

Working in the Final End

To work in the end piece:

• Insert the hook under the two loops of the next stitch from front to back, grab the end piece and then pull it all the way through. *(figure 22.1.)*

• Now from back to front, insert the hook under the two loops of the next stitch, grab the end piece and then pull it completely through. *(figure 22.2.)* Repeat these two steps five more times, then cut the end piece flush.

21.2.(above left) End about to be pulled through.

21.3. (above) End

22.2. (below) Hook inserted in next stitch, back to front.

22.1. (below) Hook inserted front to back.

 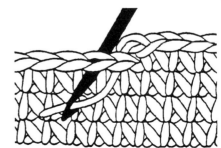

All of the projects in this book will require some *blocking*, either to flatten out a piece or to re-shape it. Blocking methods vary, depending on the dimensions of the piece.

To block a *flat* piece, first you must find a hard, flat surface, I use the floor for large pieces and an ironing board for small pieces. If you decide to use the floor, lay down a towel first, then place your piece face down. Cover the piece with a thin cotton towel. *(figure 23.)*

Blocking
Flat Pieces

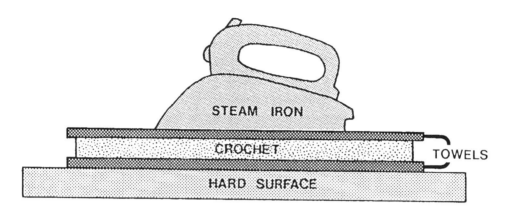

23. Blocking a flat piece.

If you are using a steam iron, fill it with water and set the iron to *steam*. If you do not have a steam iron, generously spray the towel on top of your piece with water.

If you are blocking wool, set the iron on *wool;* if you are blocking synthetic yarn be sure to set the iron on *synthetic,* because synthetics will melt at high temperatures.

Iron back and forth with a steady, downward pressure. When the piece is flat, remove the towel on top and let the piece cool off. Some pieces will require a second blocking.

Extra-large flat pieces are very difficult to block with an ordinary household iron. Some dry cleaners will block the piece for you. If the surface of the piece is very uneven, it will require several blockings to get it into shape.

To block a three-dimensional shape, such as a basket or shoulder bag, cover a can a bit smaller than the piece with a towel and insert it inside the piece. Cover the crocheted piece with a thin cotton towel. Steam the piece as previously described for flat pieces, moving the can and towel when needed. *(figure 24.)*

Blocking Three-Dimensional Pieces

Blocking
continued

For an irregular shape, such as the shaped basket, use a towel folded a couple of times supported by your hand on the inside of the piece. Steam the piece as usual, rotating it until it is completely blocked. Some pieces will require a second and third blocking.

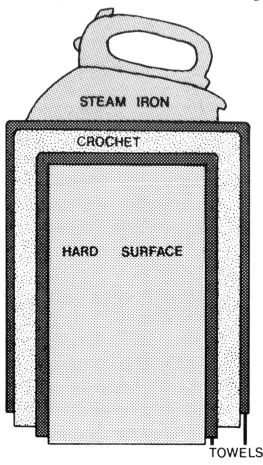

24. *Blocking a shaped piece.*

Cleaning

Depending on the fiber, tapestry crochet can be either washed or dry cleaned. Very large pieces that are too difficult to handle should be dry cleaned; small pieces can be hand washed.

Keep a record of the type of yarn used for each project so that if you decide to have them dry cleaned you can tell the dry cleaner what type of material he is dealing with. Some fibers melt at high temperature, so this is very important.

If you decide to hand wash the piece, handle it as you would a sweater. Wash it in cold or lukewarm water with a mild soap. Never leave it soaking for a long time, or it might shrink. Rinse it well, making sure that all of the soap has been removed. Roll it up in a dry bath towel and then gently squeeze to remove excess moisture. Lay the piece out on a level surface to dry and reshape if necessary. Never hang the piece up to dry, as this would stretch it out of shape. It is sometimes necessary to reblock a piece once it has dried.

3. Other Crochet Techniques

Crocheting in a Spiral

The clock faces, baskets, and cylindrical shoulder bag projects all use this technique.
To practice crocheting in a spiral:

• Make a slip knot, then chain 8 stitches.

• Form a circle by inserting the hook into the first chain stitch. Yarn over, pull through a loop of yarn, and then continue to pull it right through the loop on the hook. This is a *slip stitch.* (figure 25.1.)

• Pull the short tail of yarn as illustrated by the arrow. (figures 25.2 and 25.3.)

• Single crochet 12 stitches onto the circle. Crochet over and under the short tail as you crochet around. (figure 25.3.)

• Work the next round by inserting the hook under the top two loops of the stitch being crocheted into, as indicated by the arrow. (figure 25.4.)

25.1 (above left). Slip stitch forming ring.

25.2. (center) Short tail of yarn tucked in.

25.3. (above) First round started in ring.

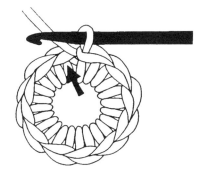

Many increases are required if a flat spiral is desired. A tube can be created by crocheting around without any increases.

25.4 Round completed.

The Double Crochet Stitch

The clock face is the only project in this book that utilizes this stitch. The *double crochet stitch* is one of three stitches that make up the scalloped border on the clock face. (See front cover and page 67.)
To start the double crochet stitch:

• Yarn over. *(figure 26.1.)*

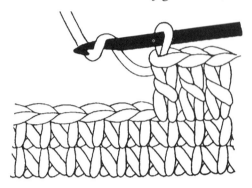
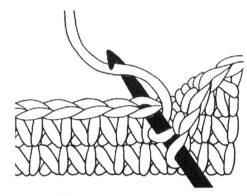

26.1. (left) Yarn over.

• Insert the hook, yarn over, and then pull through a loop. The hook now has three loops on it. *(figure 26.2.)*

26.2. Loop being pulled through.

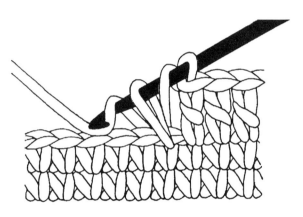

• Yarn over and then pull it through the first two loops on the hook. *(figure 26.3.)*

26.3 (left) Second stage of the stitch.

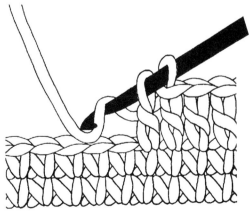
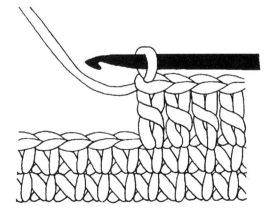

26.4. Yarn pulled through first 2 loops on hook; yarn over again.

• Yarn over again and then pull it through the remaining two loops on the hook to complete the stitch. *(figures 26.4 and 5.)*

26.5. Double crochet stitch completed.

The Triple Crochet Stitch

The *triple crochet stitch* is a tall, openwork stitch. The clock face project utilizes this stitch to form its scalloped border. See front cover and page 67.

To start the triple crochet stitch:

• Yarn over twice. *(figure 27.1.)*

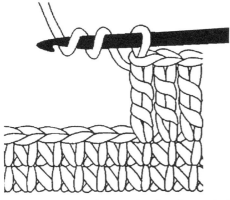

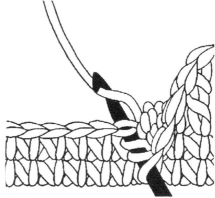

27.1 (left) Yarn over hook twice.

• Insert the hook, and then pull through a loop. The hook now has four loops on it. *(figure 27.2.)*

27.2. Thread being pulled through fabric.

•Yarn over, *(figure 27.3.)* then pull it through the first two loops, leaving three loops on the hook.

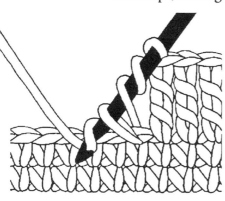

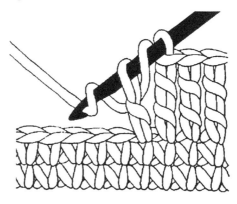

27.3. (above) Yarn over again.

• Yarn over, pull it through the next two loops. *(figure 27.4.)*

• Yarn over, pull it through the remaining two loops on the hook to complete the stitch. *(figures 27.5 and 27.6.)*

27.4. (above) Thread pulled through two loops and yarn over.

27.5. (below) Yarn over again to pull through last loop.

27.6. (below) Triple crochet stitch completed.

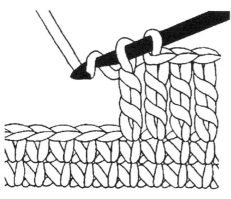

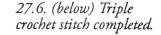

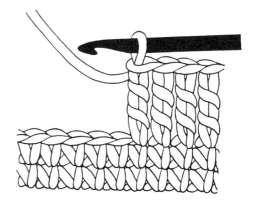

Either the *reverse single crochet* stitch, Method A, or the *alternate-row-switch-hands-single crochet* stitch, Method B, can be utilized to create the rectangular, single-faced, flat wall hangings. Both methods keep the "knot" side of the stitch on the back of the fabric, for a smoother face. Try both methods and use the one most comfortable for your working style.

To practice the *reverse single crochet* stitch:

• Make a slip knot, then chain 12 stitches.

• Single crochet eleven stitches onto the chain as you did when crocheting in rounds. Chain one stitch at the end of the row. (*figure 28.*)

• Turn the piece over. Insert the hook where the arrow indicates. (*figure 29.1.*)

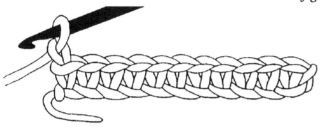

28. *First row worked in normal single crochet.*

• Insert the hook *from back to front* (*figure 29.2.*) and pull through a loop. The hook now has two loops on it.

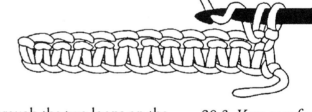

29.1. *Piece turned over.*

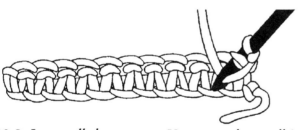

29.2. *Loop pulled through in reverse direction.*

• Yarn over, then pull it through the two loops on the hook. This completes a reverse single crochet stitch. (*figure 29.3.*)

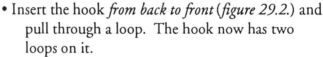

29.3. *Yarn over for first stitch.*

• Insert the hook into the next stitch where the arrow indicates, again from back to front. (*figure 29.4.*)

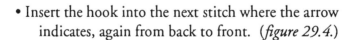

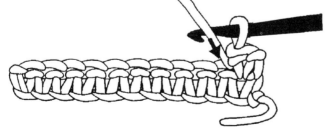

29.4. *Position of second reverse-direction stitch indicated by arrow.*

• Do the reverse single crochet stitch across the row. (*figure 29.5.*) Chain one stitch at the end of the row. Turn the piece over and then single crochet normally across the row.

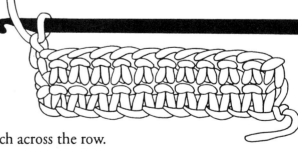

29.5. *First reverse-direction row completed.*

Alternate-Row Switch-Hands Single Crochet

Flat Method B

Either the *alternate-row switch-hands single crochet* stitch, Method B, or the *reverse single crochet* stitch, Method A can be utilized to create rectangular, single-faced, flat wall hangings. Both methods keep the "knot" side of the stitch on the back of the fabric, for a smoother face. Try both methods and use the one most comfortable for your working style.

To practice the *alternate-row-switch-hands* single crochet method:

• Make a slip knot, then chain twelve stitches.

• Single crochet eleven stitches onto the chain as you did when crocheting in rounds. Chain one stitch at the end of the row. Now, *switch hands. (figure 30.1.)* If you use your right hand to hold the hook, you will now use your left hand. If you normally hold the yarn with your left hand, you will hold it now with your right hand.

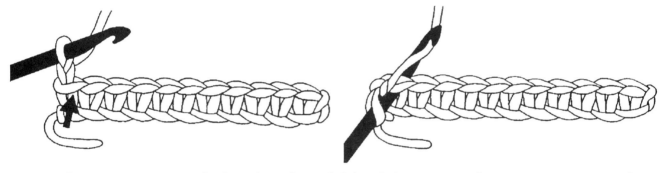

30.1. *Working direction changed by switching hands at end of row.*

Turn back to the right- or left-handed tapestry crochet instructions to review the correct technique. *If you are right-handed,* look at the *left-handed* instructions, page 24. *If you are left-handed,* look at the *right-handed* instructions, page 25. At first this technique is very awkward, but with practice you will get used to it.

• Insert the hook into the stitch indicated by the arrow.

• Insert the hook and pull through a loop. *(figure 30.2.)* The hook now has two loops on it. Yarn over, then pull it through the two loops on the hook to complete an *alternate-row-switch-hands* single crochet stitch. *(figure 30.3.)*

30.2. *First turned stitch begun.*

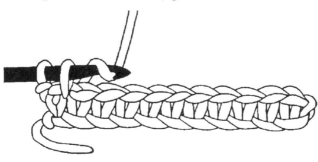

30.3. *First turned stitch in process.*

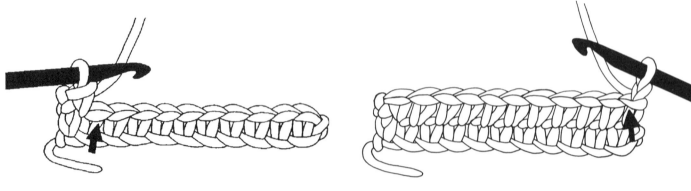

Flat Method B
continued

- Insert the hook into the next stitch where the arrow indicates. *(figure 30.4.)*

- Do the alternate-row switch-hands single crochet stitch across the row.

- Chain one stitch at the end of the row. Switch hands again. Insert the hook where the arrow indicates and single crochet normally across the row. *(figure 30.5.)*

30.4. (left) First turned stitch completed, Arrow indicates next stitch.

30.5. (above) First row of alternate-row-switch-hands single crochet completed.

Crocheting a Border

The flat wall hangings in this book have a simple single crocheted border to give them a more finished look. Practice crocheting a border around one of your sample pieces. Use the *reverse single crochet* or the *alternate-row-switch-hands single crochet* sample for experimenting with borders.

To work a border:

- Single crochet across the top of the piece.

- Single crochet three stitches into the first corner stitch. *(figure 31.)*

To turn the corner:

- Turn the piece around a quarter of the way (45°) until the left side is on the top. Insert the hook into the space at the end of the row indicated by the arrow for the next stitch.

- Continue to single crochet across the side of the piece, inserting the hook into the spaces at the end of each row.

Depending upon your tension, one single crochet stitch per row is about right. If the piece starts to pucker, increase a stitch or two along the border. If the piece starts to look wavy, decrease a stitch or two along the border.

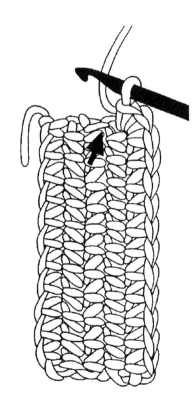

31. Border in process. Three stitches made in corner stitch.

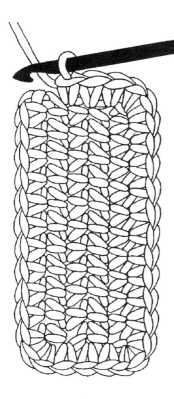

32. Border completed.

To turn the next corner:

• Single crochet three stitches into the corner stitch.

• Turn the piece 45° again so that the bottom of the piece is now on the top.

• Continue to single crochet across, inserting the hook into the bottom loop of the original foundation chain. Carry the tail piece along and crochet over it to hide and secure it.

• At the next corner, single crochet three stitches into the corner stitch.

• Turn the piece 45°, then continue to single crochet across the side of the piece as on the previous side.

• Single crochet three stitches into the last corner stitch, then start a second round of border stitches. *(figure 32.)*

   The border can be stopped here with a slip stitch, or continued indefinitely by single crocheting one stitch into every single crochet stitch, and three single crochet stitches into each corner stitch. You might try a tapestry crochet border, or create a wide frame by crocheting a number of border rows with various colors and textures of yarns. A *raised border* will result if only one stitch is worked into the corner stitch.

Photo 8. Detail of a tapestry crochet shoulder bag designed by the author. The entire bag is shown in Photo 2.

4. Design

Each project in this book features a different aspect of the tapestry crochet technique. By working through the series of projects presented in the following chapters, you will develop a foundation that will allow you to develop your own designs.

I have taken an exact, horizontal approach to tapestry crochet in this book. However, one of the fantastic advantages of crochet is that any shape can be executed whether flat or three-dimensional. What about an oval, triangular, or square basket. . . a three-dimensional or textured wall tapestry? Other possibilities include coasters, pot holders, napkin rings, placemats, rugs, afghans, shoes or slippers, belts, bags, hats, a coat or vest, Christmas or Hanukkah decorations, toys, a lampshade and base, guitar straps, book covers, free-standing sculptures... the list is as endless as your imagination.

A number of other crochet stitches can be incorporated in addition to the single crochet stitch. It all depends upon the look that you are trying to achieve and your creativity.

Design Sources

Many existing crafts, such as needlepoint, knitting, and embroidery use motifs that can easily be transferred to tapestry crochet graphs. Many cultures use design motifs that can be translated into tapestry crochet graphs. A trip to a museum of folk art or natural history will provide many design ideas. Nature is a primary source of design and color inspiration.

Use of Color

As many different-colored yarns as you can handle can be incorporated into a piece. Since the yarns will twist around one another as the colors are switched, try not to work with more than three yarns at one time. This avoids tall stitches and a tangled mess of yarns. Through careful planning, a number of colors can be used for the piece even though only three are being crocheted at any one time. The "...I still have a dream..." tapestry shown in *Plates 18 and 19* is a good example of careful planning and spacing of colors.

If three yarns are required for only a portion of a project, they should be carried throughout the piece from the beginning, even if they will not be immediately utilized, to assure a consistent, unwarped result. If each color is introduced as needed, the piece will appear lumpy because stitches made over the additional carried yarns will be larger. An uneven appearance may be desirable for a particular piece – it is up to you.

Using Tapestry Crochet Graph Papers

After you have decided what item you want to crochet, think about the design motif. Four tapestry crochet graph papers are included on pages 43 - 46. *For working in rounds,* use graph paper *#1R,* if you are right-handed, or *#1L* if you are left-handed. *To design a flat piece,* use graph paper *#2A or #2B,* depending on the size of the stitches. *Graph paper #2B* is designed for a taller stitch height, the result of carrying more yarns.

Use a pencil to sketch in a variety of motifs on a photocopy of the graph paper most appropriate for your project.

These crochet grid graph papers take into consideration *actual stitch placement.* Crochet a small sample piece if the planned motif has to be precise. The actual stitch height, or the *rows per inch measurement,* will depend on the yarn, tension, and the number of carried yarns. The stitch height can significantly affect the proportion of the finished motif.

Design Aids

A computer can be an ideal tool for designing tapestry crochet motifs, because it can be programmed with a special graph paper which can be adjusted in height or width to meet the needs of various projects. Graph paper *#2B* was developed in this way.

Graph Paper #1L (for left-handed tapestry crochet worked in rounds). ©1984 C. Norton

Graph Paper #1R (for right-handed tapestry crochet). ©1984 C. Norton

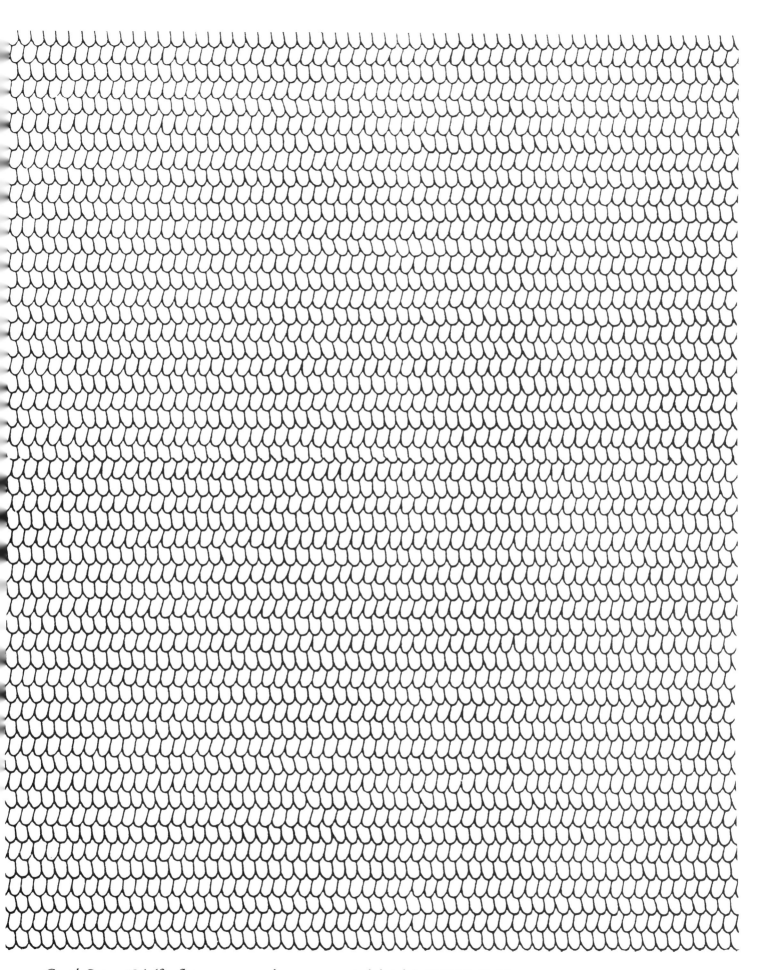

Graph Paper #2A (for flat tapestry crochet, average stitch height). ©1985 C. Norton

45

Graph Paper #2B (for flat tapestry crochet, taller stitch height from carrying several yarns). © 1985 C. Norton.

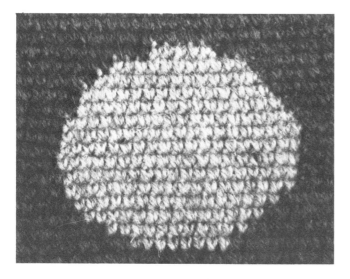

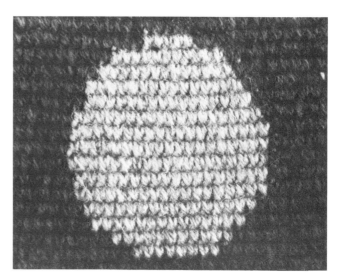

Photo 9. (above) Circle motif crocheted in rounds, one yarn carried.

Photo 10. (above right) Circle motif crocheted in rounds, two yarns carried. Note the difference in stitch height.

In the circle motif crocheted in rounds shown in *Photo 9*, each stitch falls slightly to one side of a stitch in the previous row; the stitches do not align directly over one another. This is a very important consideration when charting a design motif.

Figure 33 shows a circle with the center filled in drawn on #1R graph paper. Where the circle intersected a stitch unit, a decision was made whether or not to fill in that stitch. *Figure 34* shows the circle motif from the #1R graph paper transferred onto regular square-ruled paper.

The circle motif crocheted in rounds shown in *Photo 9* resulted from carrying one yarn. A rounder circle could have been made by decreasing the number of stitches across the diameter.

The circle motif crocheted in rounds shown in *Photo 10* resulted from carrying two yarns. Notice the taller stitch created by the extra bulk of the second carried yarn.

Circle Motif Worked in Rounds

33. Circle drawn on Graph Paper #1R.

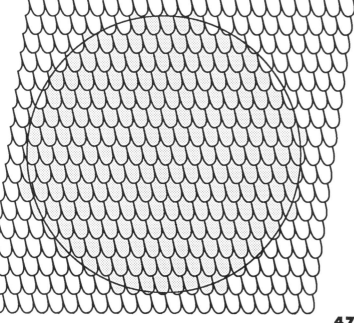

34. Circle motif drawn on square-ruled paper.

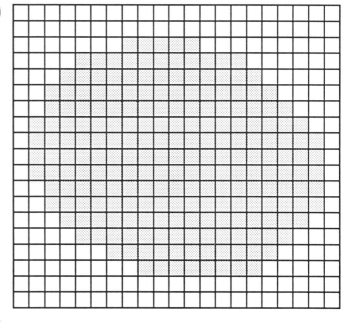

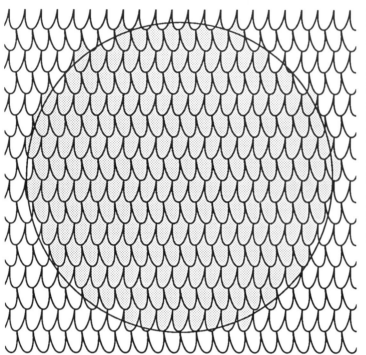

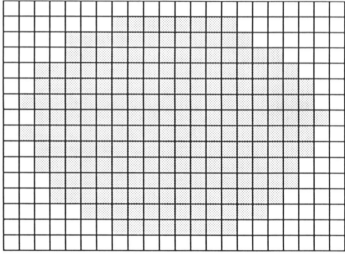

The stitch configuration is different for a piece worked in the round than for a flat piece. The circle motif shown in *Photo 11* is crocheted back and forth. On one row, all of the stitches slant to the right, on the next row they all slant to the left. Graph papers *2A* and *2B* have been designed for flat tapestry crochet work and are different than graph paper *#1* for this reason.

   Figure 35 shows a circle motif with the center filled in, drawn on graph paper #2A. Where the outline of the circle intersected a stitch block, a decision was made whether or not to fill in that stitch to achieve a curved outline.

   Figure 36 shows the circle motif from graph paper #2A transferred onto square-ruled graph paper for ease in counting stitches.

   Compare *Photos 11* and *12* on the next page. The circle motif crocheted back and forth shown in *Photo 12* resulted from carrying two yarns. Notice the taller stitch created by the extra bulk of the second carried yarn.

35. (above left) Circle on #2A Graph paper for working back and forth.

36. (above) Flat circle motif transferred to square-ruled paper. Note distortion of pattern.

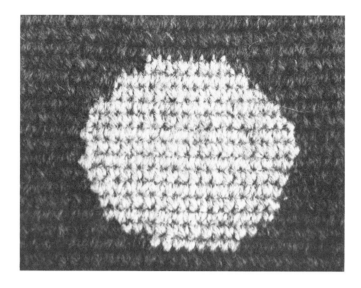

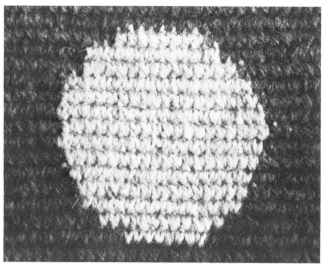

Photo 11. (above) Circle motif crocheted back and forth, one yarn carried.

Photo 12. (above right) Circle motif crocheted back and forth, two yarns carried.

Charting the Design

After the motif has been worked out on either graph paper *#1* or *#2*, it should be transferred to square-ruled graph paper. The eye perceives stitch placement much more clearly on ruled graph paper, making it easier to count stitches and determine color changes.

Be especially careful when transferring a motif from crochet graph paper #2. It is crucial to understand the vertical stitch placement of graph paper *#2* in relation to the square-ruled paper, which does not show the true stitch height-to-width proportion. Study the circle motif on graph paper *#2* as compared to the square-ruled sample. See *figures 35* and *36*.

The next step is to count the number of horizontal stitches in the motif. The base of the piece should be a multiple of the horizontal measurement. For instance, the triangular motif in the *Baskets* project on page 72 has twelve horizontal stitches. If the number of stitches of the base is divisible by twelve, the motif can be started at any point.

37. Design charted on Graph Paper #2.

38. Design transferred to square-ruled graph paper.

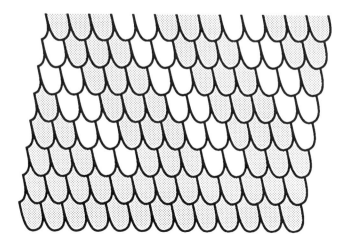

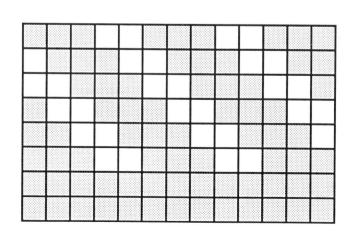

The *Shaped Basket with Lid* project's pattern on page 83 has eighteen stitches in its horizontal measurement, which means that the motif can only be started when a round has a number divisible by eighteen. I decided to start the motif when the base had 180 stitches. If I had started on the previous row, which only had 168 stitches I would have had twelve stitches left over at the end of the round

Interpreting the Charted Illustrations

Each square or shell-shape on the various graph papers represents a single tapestry crochet stitch. The dark squares or shells represent a dark-colored yarn and the white squares or shells represent white, or light-colored yarn. All of the charted patterns are read from the bottom up. *(figures 37 and 38.)*

The charted motifs included for each project are drawn for right-handed crocheters. Photos are of right-handed work. Left-handed crocheters should place a mirror to the side of the illustrations and photographs and then read the mirror image.

Graph paper #1 for crocheting in rounds is read from right to left, if you are a right-handed crocheter. The mirror image is read from left to right if you are a left-handed crocheter.

Graph paper #2 for flat tapestries is read alternately from right to left and then from left to right, which corresponds to the back-and-forth crocheting technique.

Project Instructions

Two graphs are provided for each project: one actual stitch placement graph on crochet *Graph Paper #1,* and the design transferred to square-ruled graph paper (labelled *S*).

Each row of instructions is also written out. Begin to work from the row-by-row directions, to see how they relate to the graphs. Eventually, you will be able to work from the graphs alone.

Plate 1. (above) Guatemalan shoulder bags made for the tourist market by men of the village of Aguacatan. Traditional bag colors and shapes have been modified to appeal to the tourist market.

Plate 2. (right) A Maya Indian man from the Guatemalan village of San Juan Atitlán crochets a shoulder bag as his wife looks on.

Plate 3. (below) Traditional Guatemalan shoulder bags, each with a distinct regional design and color scheme. From left to right, bags are from the villages of Todos Santos, Nebaj, Aguacatan and San Juan Atitlán.

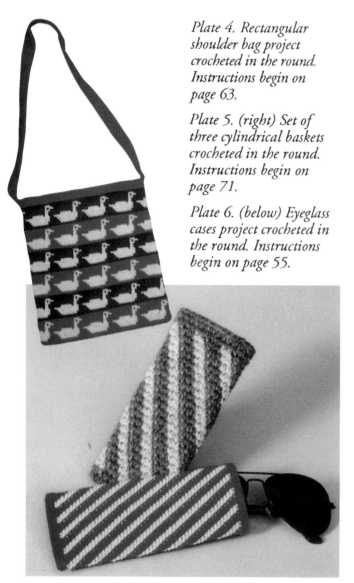

Plate 4. Rectangular shoulder bag project crocheted in the round. Instructions begin on page 63.

Plate 5. (right) Set of three cylindrical baskets crocheted in the round. Instructions begin on page 71.

Plate 6. (below) Eyeglass cases project crocheted in the round. Instructions begin on page 55.

Plate 7. (above) Change purses project crocheted in the round. Purses are flat or 3-dimensional depending on placement of zipper. Instructions begin on page 57.

Plate 8. (above right) Cylindrical shoulder bags project crocheted in the round. Instructions begin on page 75.

Plate 9. (right) Tapestry crochet pillow project crocheted in the round. Instructions begin on page 59.

Plate 10. (left) Clock face project. Instructions begin on page 67.

Plate 11. (above) Wall hanging project designed from a photograph. Instructions begin on page 90.

Plate 12. Shoulder bags with experimental design described in the Introduction. This design inspired the wall hanging in Plate 18.

Plate 13. Shaped basket with lid project. Instructions begin on page 81.

Plate 14. A variety of shaped baskets based on pojects in this book. From left to right: basket in bulky wool carpet yarn, shaped basket in 4-ply synthetic yarn,

Plate 15. "Someday..." wall hanging project in flat tapestry crochet. Instructions begin on page 87.

Plate 16. (below) Detail, "Stop...Genocide..." with bronze hand. Full view is in Plate 17.

MARTIN LUTHER KING 1929-68

Plate 17. (above) "Stop...Genocide..." (1985) tapestry crochet wall hanging by the author. This 61" x 86" x 5" tapestry is about the struggle in Central America. The figure has been backed against the wall, then into it, a gun pointed at his heart. Two bronze hands and a foot are bolted through the tapestry to the wall.

Plate 18. (left) "...I Still Have a Dream..." (1983) wall hanging by the author. This fine-gauge 27" x 56" crocheted tapestry pays homage to Dr. Martin Luther King. The light blue background symbolizes sky and water, the green symbolizes the land that both unites and separates us. Rows of people of different races hold hands to depict world unity, with hearts for friendship and love. Plate 19. (below) Detail of figures.

These attractive eyeglass cases take full advantage of the heavy, protective fabric made with tapestry crochet. See *Plate 6*. Techniques introduced include: the slip knot and chain stitch, single crochet worked in rounds, counting stitches, carrying a yarn of a different color, and working the tapestry crochet stitch. You will also interpret a graph paper design, check your gauge, cut the yarn flush, finish off a piece, work in the yarn end, and block the finished piece.

Both eyeglass cases follow the same graph paper design. Follow the specific instructions in ( ) for the modacrylic yarn eyeglass case.

Rectangular Eyeglass Cases

Eyeglass Case #1
(foreground):

Size
2½" wide by 6" high

Materials
8 Cord Cable Crochet Cotton (the heaviest Crochet Cotton sold), ⅔ ounce of white and ⅔ ounce of color;

steel hook #6 or the size that will give an acceptable gauge.

Gauge
10 stitches = 1 inch,
9 rows = 1 inch.

Photo 13. Eyeglass Cases. Foreground, Case #1 in cotton yarn. Rear, Case #2 in modacrylic. Both cases are worked from the same graphed design.

Eyeglass Case #2
(back):

Size
3" wide by 6¼" high

Materials
Modacrylic three-ply carpet yarn or a similar substitute,
1 ounce of white and 1 ounce of color;

aluminum crochet hook size E or the size that will give an acceptable gauge.

Gauge
5 stitches = 1 inch,
4½ rows = 1 inch.

Round 1: Make a slip knot with the colored yarn, then chain 25 in crochet cotton, or 15 stitches in modacrylic carpet yarn. Increase or decrease in multiples of 5 chain stitches at this point to make a larger or smaller eyeglass case.

Round 2: Starting with the second chain, single crochet 24 cotton (14 modacrylic) stitches. Single crochet 2 more stitches into the last chain for a total of 26 cotton (16 modacrylic) stitches. Continue to single crochet using the new top of the chain until you come around to the first stitch. This first round should have a total of 29 cotton (29 modacrylic) stitches. Slip a safety pin into the last stitch if you want to keep track of where each round ends. Remove the safety pin from the last stitch as you come to it again and slip it into the new last stitch.

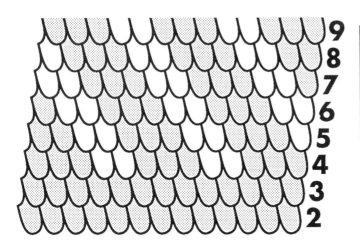

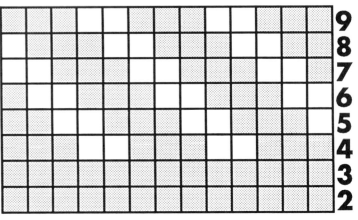

Graph 1S

Photo 14. Detail, face of the modacrylic eyeglass case.

Round 3: Start to carry the white yarn. Single crochet a colored round. The case should still have 49 cotton (29 modacrylic) stitches when you finish this round

Round 4: Start the diagonal stripe pattern as follows: tapestry crochet 3 stitches with color, and then tapestry crochet 2 white stitches. Repeat this sequence 9 more times with the cotton (5 more times with the modacrylic). Turn the eyeglass case right side out. The side facing you as you crochet is the right side.

Round 5 and subsequent rounds: Continue to tapestry crochet the pattern, 3 color, then 2 white stitches, until the eyeglass case measures 5 3/4 inches long, or longer if desired.

Last Rounds: Single crochet 2 rounds with color. Continue to carry the white until the last 3 single crochet stitches. Cut the white yarn flush. Single crochet the last 3 color stitches.

Finish off. Work in the end. Block the finished eyeglass case.

Photo 15. Detail, Reverse of the modacrylic eyeglass case.

Photo 16. Detail, Face of the cotton eyeglass case.

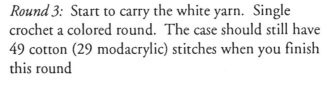

These unique change purses are worked from the same pattern graphs as the eyeglass cases. See *Plate 7*. This project will teach you how to vary the size and how to sew in a zipper. A flat or three-dimensional change purse is possible, depending upon how the zipper is sewn in.

Follow the instructions in ( ) for the larger change purse worked in modacrylic yarn.

Change Purses

Purse #1

Size

without zipper:
3¼" wide by 3" high

Materials

8 cord cable crochet cotton (the heaviest crochet cotton sold), ¼ ounce of white and ½ ounce of color;

steel crochet hook #6 or the size that will give an acceptable gauge;

4" nylon zipper or a longer one which may be cut down; invisible thread.

Gauge

10 stitches = 1 inch, 9 rows = 1 inch

Photo 17. Change purses: left, 3-dimensional purses in cotton and modacrylic yarns. Right, flat purse in cotton. See photos 14-16 fabric texture.

Round 1: Starting with the color yarn, make a slip knot, then chain 35 stitches in crochet cotton (25 stitches in modacrylic carpet yarn). Increase or decrease in multiples of 5 chain stitches at this point to make a larger or smaller change purse.

Round 2: Starting with the second chain, single crochet 34 cotton (24 modacrylic) stitches. Single crochet 2 more stitches into the last chain for a total of 36 cotton (26 modacrylic) stitches. Continue to single crochet using the new top of the chain until you come around to the first stitch. The change purse should have a total of 69 cotton (49 modacrylic) stitches. Slip a safety pin into the last stitch, if you want to keep track of where each round ends. Remove the safety pin from the last stitch as you come to it again and slip it into the new last stitch.

Round 3: Start to carry the white yarn. Single crochet a plain round. The change purse should still have 69 cotton (49 modacrylic) stitches when you finish this round.

Purse #2

Size

without zipper:
4½" wide by 4" high

Materials

Modacrylic three-ply carpet yarn or a similar substitute,
One ounce of white and one ounce of color;

aluminum crochet hook size E, or size that will give an acceptable gauge;

5" nylon or metal zipper or a longer one which may be cut down; invisible nylon thread.

Gauge

5½ stitches = 1 inch, 5 rows = 1 inch.

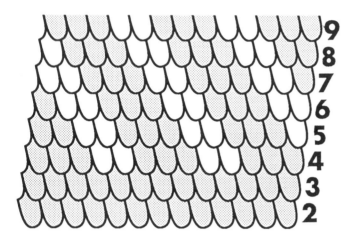

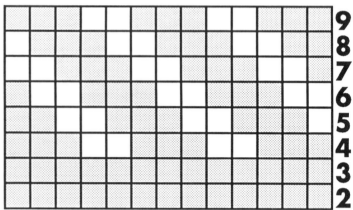

Graph 2

Graph 2S

Round 4 Start the diagonal stripe pattern as follows: tapestry crochet 3 stitches with color, then 2 white stitches. Repeat this sequence 13 more times with the cotton (9 more times with the modacrylic). Turn the change purse right side out. The side facing you as you crochet is the right side.

Round 5: Continue to tapestry crochet the pattern, 3 color then 2 white stitches, until the change purse measures 2 3/4" (3 1/2") high, or higher if desired.

Last Rounds: Single crochet the last two rounds with color. Continue to carry the white until the last 3 single crochet stitches. Cut the white yarn flush. Single crochet the last 3 color stitches. Finish off. Work in the end. Block the change purse.

Finishing Sew in the zipper as follows:

1) If the zipper is too long, measure from the top of the zipper down to as long as you need it to be. Sew back and forth to create a "lock" as in figure 39. Cut off the lower portion of the zipper, leaving 3/4" piece below the sewn lock.

2) Open the zipper, and baste (hand sew with large stitches) the zipper into the change purse.

3) With invisible thread, either hand sew with small stitches or machine sew the zipper into the change purse.

4) Remove the basting.

5) Block the change purse again.

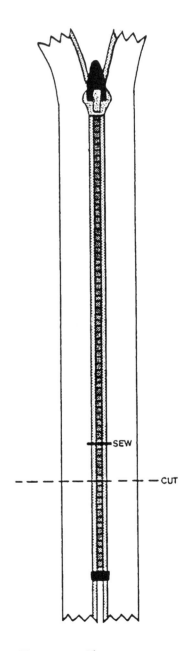

Figure 39. Shortening the zipper.

What could be more attractive than a tapestry crochet pillow? Feel free to use colors that coordinate with your decor. Perhaps you could even substitute your own original motif for the one in *Graph 3*.

This project was designed to familiarize you with a more complex graph paper design. See *Plate 9*. You will also learn how to stuff the pillow, and how to sew together the top seam.

Pillow

Pillow

Size
13½" wide by 12½" high

Materials
4-ply worsted weight acrylic fiber yarn or a similar substitue, 5 ounces of white and 8 ounces of color;

17 ounces of 100% polyester fiber;

aluminum crochet hook size C or the size that will give an acceptable gauge;

tapestry sewing needle.

Gauge
7 stitches = 1 inch, 6 rows = 1 inch.

Photo 18. Tapestry crochet pillow with deer motif.

Round 1: Make a slip knot starting with the color yarn, then chain 96 stitches. Increase or decrease in multiples of 6 at this point if you want a wider or narrower pillow.

Round 2: Starting with the second chain, single crochet 95 stitches. Single crochet 2 more stitches into the last chain for a total of 97 stitches. Continue to single crochet using the new top of the chain until you come around to the first stitch. Single crochet 1 more stitch into the last stitch. You should have a total of 192 stitches when you finish this round. Slip a safety pin into the last stitch if you want to keep track of where each round ends. Remove the safety pin from the last stitch as you come to it again and slip it into the new last stitch.

Round 3: Start to carry the white yarn. Single crochet a plain round. The pillow should still have 192 stitches when you finish this round.

Round 4: Start the deer motif *(Graph 3S)* as follows: tapestry crochet 2 white, 4 color, 2 white, 4 color stitches. Repeat this sequence 15 more times.

59

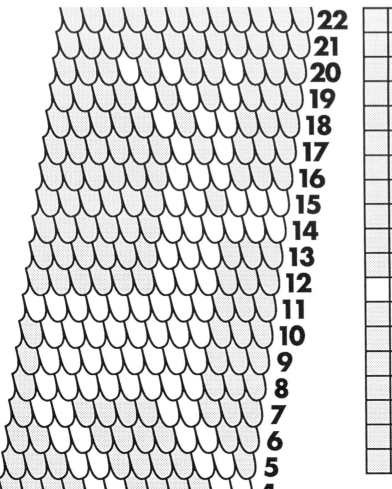

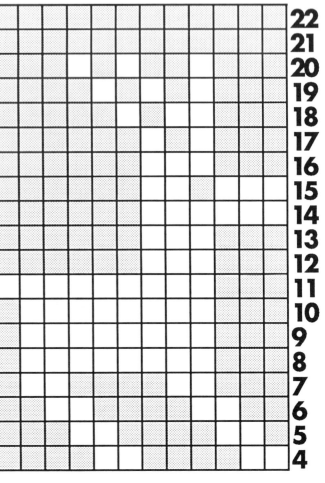

Graph 3.

Round 5: Tapestry crochet 1 color, 2 white, 4 color, 2 white, 3 color stitches. Repeat this sequence 15 more times.

Round 6: Tapestry crochet 2 color, 2 white, 4 color, 2 white, 2 color stitches. Repeat around.

Graph 3S.

Photo 19. Detail, face of deer motif.

Photo 20. Detail, reverse side of deer motif.

60

Round 7: Tapestry crochet 3 color, 2 white, 4 color, 2 white, 1 color stitch. Repeat around.

Rounds 8, 9, and 10: Tapestry crochet 3 color, 8 white, 1 color stitch. Repeat around.

Round 11: Tapestry crochet 3 color, 9 white stitches. Repeat around.

Rounds 12 and 13: Tapestry crochet 3 color, 3 white, 6 color stitches. Repeat around.

Round 14: Tapestry crochet 6 white, 6 color stitches. Repeat around.

Round 15: Tapestry crochet 3 white, 1 color, 2 white, 6 color stitches. Repeat around.

Round 16: Tapestry crochet 3 color, 3 white, 6 color stitches. Repeat around.

Round 17: Tapestry crochet 3 color, 1 white, 1 color, 1 white, 6 color stitches. Repeat around.

Round 18: Tapestry crochet 3 color, 2 white, 1 color, 1 white, 5 color stitches. Repeat around.

Round 19: Tapestry crochet 3 color, 1 white, 1 color, 1 white, 1 color, 1 white, 4 color stitches. Repeat around.

Round 20: Tapestry crochet 3 color, 1 white, 2 color, 1 white, 1 color, 1 white, 3 color stitches. Repeat around.

Rounds 21 and 22: Single crochet a plain round of color stitches, continuously carrying the white.

Repeat rounds 4 through 22 three more times. Continue to carry the white yarn until you reach the last three stitches of the pillow. Cut the white yarn flush. Single crochet the last three color stitches.

Finishing

Finish off. Work in the end. Block the pillow. Sew the top and stuff the pillow as follows:

• Cut a seven-foot piece of colored yarn and thread it through the tapestry needle.

• Attach the yarn starting at the top right corner of the pillow, by pushing the needle from the inside through the top two loops of one of the first single crochet stitches to the far right.

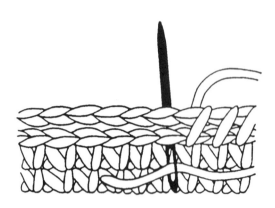

40. Sewing the seam.

- Pull the yarn through the loops, leaving a two-inch tail.
- Insert the needle from the outside through the top two loops of the single crochet stitch into the pillow, facing the stitch you just used. Knot the two ends of yarn together.

- From front to back, insert the needle into the top two loops of the next single crochet stitches facing each other. Pull the yarn through. *(figure 40.)*

- Repeat this stitch until only four inches of the pillow are left to be sewn.

- Stuff the pillow, making sure that the stuffing gets into the corners.

- Continue to sew the pillow adding bits of stuffing as you go.

- When you have finished sewing across the top of the pillow, sew a couple of stitches into the last stitch.

- Insert the needle under the last six stitches and then pull the yarn through.

- Cut the yarn flush.

- Punch the pillow all over to distribute the stuffing.

This three-color rectangular shoulder bag, inspired by its Guatemalan counterparts, is worked in a manner similar to the pillow project. The design is worked from *Graph 4*. See *Plate 4*.

This project will teach you how to alternate the background color and how to crochet a shoulder strap.

Rectangular Shoulder Bag

Size
9½" wide by
10½" high
(not including strap)

Materials
4-ply Wintuk Knitting Worsted (orlon acrylic) or a similar substitute, 3½ ounces of color A, 3½ ounces of white, and 2 ounces of color B;

aluminum crochet hook size C or the size that will give an acceptable gauge.

Gauge
7½ stitches = 1 inch,
6½ rows = 1 inch.

Photo 21. Rectangular shoulder bag with duck motif and a crocheted strap. The background color alternates in bands

Round 1: Starting with color A, make a slip knot, then chain 72 stitches. Add or decrease stitches in multiples of 8 at this point to make a wider or narrower shoulder bag.

Round 2: Starting with the second chain, single crochet 71 stitches. Single crochet 2 more stitches into the last chain for a total of 73 stitches. Continue to single crochet using the new top of the chain until you come around to the first stitch of this round. Single crochet 1 more stitch into the last stitch. You should have a total of 144 stitches. Slip a safety pin into the last stitch if you want to keep track of where each round ends. Remove the safety pin from the last stitch as you come to it again, and slip it into the new last stitch.

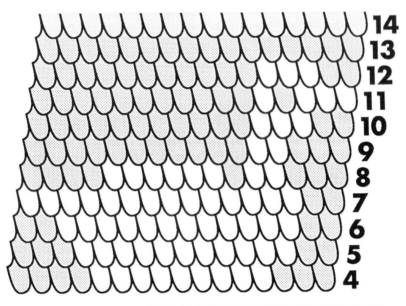

Graph 4.

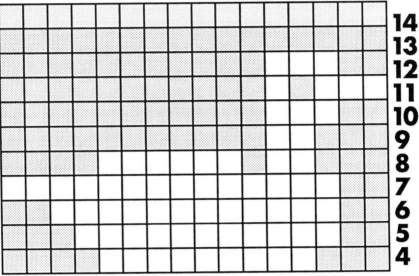

Graph 4S

Round 3: Start to carry the white yarn. Single crochet a plain round with the color yarn. There should still be 144 stitches when you finish this round.

Round 4: Start the duck motif as follows: tapestry crochet 3 color, 9 white, 4 color stitches. Repeat this sequence 8 more time.

Round 5: Tapestry crochet 2 color, 11 white, 3 color stitches. Repeat this sequence 8 more times.

Round 6: Tapestry crochet 2 color, 12 white, 2 color stitches. Repeat around.

Round 7: Tapestry crochet 2 color, 14 white stitches. Repeat around.

Round 8: Tapestry crochet 3 color, 2 white, 1 color, 6 white, 4 color stitches. Repeat around.

Photo 21. Detail, face of the duck motif shoulder bag.

Round 9: Tapestry crochet 3 color, 2 white, 11 color stitches. Repeat around.

Round 10: Tapestry crochet 2 color, 3 white, 11 color stitches. Repeat around.

Round 11: Tapestry crochet 3 white, 1 color, 1 white, 11 color stitches. Repeat around.

Round 12: Tapestry crochet 2 color, 3 white, 11 color stitches. Repeat around.

Round 13: Single crochet a plain round of color stitches continuously carrying the white. Start to carry the other color yarn for the last 10 stitches of this round.

Round 14: Continue carrying white and previous color yarn. Single crochet 10 stitches with the new color. Cut the previous color yarn flush. Continue to carry the white yarn and single crochet around with the new color yarn.

Repeat rounds 4 through 14 five more times.

Border of bag and strap are worked together.
A: Single crochet 11 color stitches. Cut the white yarn flush. Chain 175 stitches with the color yarn. If you would like a longer or shorter shoulder strap, increase or decrease at this point. Insert the hook into the 73rd stitch away from the base of the chain, connecting the end of the chain to the other side of the top of the shoulder bag. Make sure that the chain is not twisted. *(figure 41.)*

Photo 22. Detail, reverse side of the duck motif shoulder bag.

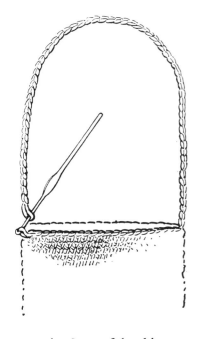

41. Start of shoulder strap.

Shoulder Strap
First half

Rectangular Shoulder Bag
continued

B: Start to carry the white yarn. Single crochet 72 stitches across the top of the bag with the color yarn. Continue to single crochet onto the chain. You should have 247 stitches when you finish this round (half of bag plus chain).

C: Single crochet 247 stitches around with the color yarn, always carrying the white yarn.

D: Single crochet 244 stitches around with the color yarn, then cut the white yarn flush. Finish off. Work in the end.

Shoulder Strap Second half

E: Turn over the shoulder bag. Have the side facing you with only two rows of color over the duck motif. Insert the hook into the stitch in the upper right hand corner of the bag next to the shoulder strap. Pull through a loop of color yarn, leaving a two-inch piece hanging out of the back. Chain 1 with the color, then single crochet 1 stitch into the same stitch. Start to carry the white yarn along with the two-inch piece of background yarn. Single crochet 71 more stitches across the top of the shoulder bag. Continue to single crochet onto the shoulder strap, inserting the hook into the bottom loops of the original chain.

F: Repeat Round C.

G: Repeat Round D.

Finishing

Block the shoulder bag.

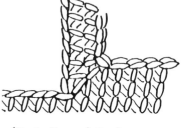

42. A, B, and C of first half of border and strap.

6. Spiral Crochet Projects

The clock face is crocheted in a flat spiral. In this project, you will also learn how to crochet a scalloped border. See *Plate 10* and front cover.

These unusual clock faces are only possible with a tight tapestry crochet stitch and acrylic carpet or rug yarn. Once blocked, they are stiff enough to support themselves. If you would like additional stiffening, back the clock face with a cardboard circle. The donkey motif in *Graph 4* is based on a Guatemalan design.

Both of the clock faces are worked from the same instructions and graphs. *Clock face #2* is worked with a finer yarn. Clock works are available in kit form. See *Suppliers List.*

Clock Faces

Clock Face #1

Size
12" diameter

Materials
Modacrylic three-ply carpet yarn or a similar substitute,
3 ounces of white and 3 ounces of color;

aluminum crochet hook size D or the size that will give an acceptable gauge;

1 battery-operated clock kit.

Gauge
5 stitches = 1 inch,
5 rows = 1 inch.

Photo 24. Clock faces: left, Clock face #2 in modacrylic yarn; right, Clock Face #1 in polypropylene rug yarn.

Round 1: Starting with the white yarn, make a slip knot, then chain 8 stitches. Join the ends together to form a ring by working a slip stitch into the first chain.

Round 2: Single crochet 12 stitches into the ring. The clock face should have a total of 12 stitches when you finish this round. Slip a safety pin into the last stitch if you want to keep track of where each round ends. Remove the safety pin from the last stitch as you come to it again, and slip it into the new last stitch.

Clock Face #2

Size
10" diameter

Materials
Heavy 100% polypropylene rug yarn or a suitable substitute,
2½ ounces of white and 1 ounce of color;

aluminum crochet hook size C or the size that will give you an acceptable guage;

1 battery-operated clock kit.

Gauge
7 stitches = 1 inch,
6 rows = 1 inch.

Clock Faces
continued

Round 3: Start to carry the color yarn. Increase in every stitch to 24 stitches in the round.

Round 4: Increase in every second stitch to 36 stitches in the round.

Round 5: Single crochet one round without any increases.

Round 6: Increase in every third stitch. The clock face should have 36 stitches when you finish this round.

Round 7: Single crochet one round without any increases.

Round 8: Increase in every fourth stitch to 60 stitches in the round.

Round 9: Increase in every fifth stitch to 72 stitches in the round.

Round 10: Single crochet one round without any increases.

Round 11: Increase in every sixth stitch to 84 stitches.

Round 12: Increase in every seventh stitch. The clock face should have 96 stitches when your finish this round

Round 13: In this round start the donkey motif as follows *(Graph 4S)*: increase in the first stitch with white, tapestry crochet 1 color, 4 white, 1 color, 1 white stitch. Repeat this sequence 11 more times. The clock face should have 108 stitches when you finish this round.

Photo 25. Detail, front of clock face.

Photo 26. Detail, reverse side of clock face.

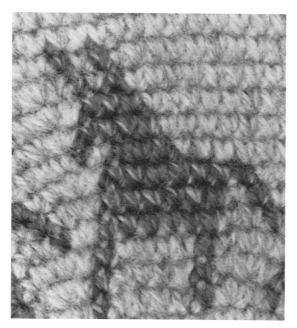

68

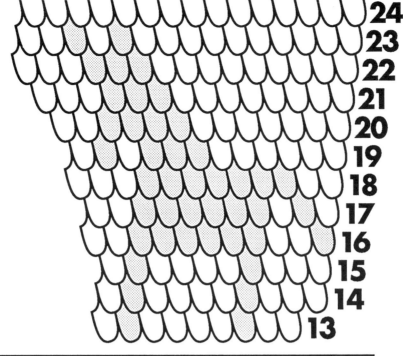

Graph 4.

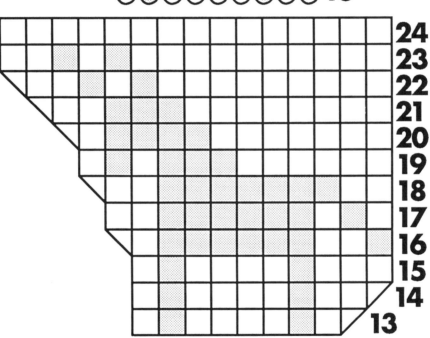

Graph 4S.

Round 14: Increase in the first stitch with white, tapestry crochet 1 white, 1 color, 4 white, 1 color, 1 white stitch. Repeat this sequence 11 more times. The clock face should now have 120 stitches.

Round 15: Tapestry crochet 3 white, 1 color, 4 white, 1 color, 1 color stitch. Repeat around.

Round 16: Tapestry crochet 1 color, 2 white, 6 color, and the increase with white. Repeat around. The clock face should now have 132 stitches.

Round 17: Tapestry crochet 1 white, 1 color, 1 white, 6 color, 2 white stitches. Repeat around.

69

Clock Faces
continued

Round 18: Tapestry crochet 2 white, 7 color, 1 white, then increase with white. Repeat around. The clock face should now have 144 stitches.

Round 19: Tapestry crochet 6 white, 3 color, 1 white, 1 color, 1 white stitch. Repeat around.

Round 20: Tapestry crochet 7 white, 4 color, then increase with white. Repeat around. The clock face should now have 156 stitches.

Round 21: Tapestry crochet 8 white, 3 color, 1 white, then increase with white. Repeat around. The clock face should now have 168 stitches.

Round 22: Tapestry crochet 9 white, 1 color, 1 white, 1 color, 1 white, then increase with white. Repeat around. The clock face should now have 180 stitches.

Round 23: Tapestry crochet 10 white, 1 color, 1 white, 1 color, and then 2 white stitches. Repeat around.

Rounds 24 and 25: Single crochet a plain round of white stitches, continuously carrying the color yarn.

Border

Round 26: With the color yarn, do 1 single crochet, 1 double crochet, 2 triple crochet, 1 double crochet, and then 1 single crochet stitch. Repeat this sequence 28 more times. Cut the white yarn flush. Finish the last sequence. Finish off. Work in the end.

Finishing

Block the clock face. If the clock face is not stiff after blocking, glue a cardboard backing onto it with white glue.

Add the clock parts to the face following the instructions in the clock kit.

Photo 27. Detail, single, double and triple crochet stitches in clock border.

Each of these baskets begins with a flat spiral base. When the diameter is no longer increased, sides of the basket will form. See *Plate 5*.

The triangular motifs on these baskets are composed of twelve stitches each. The base of each basket is a multiple of twelve, so it is possible to make a variety of baskets with the same design motif simply by increasing or decreasing the size of the base. Three sizes are included here.

Cylindrical Baskets

Small Basket

Size
3" diameter by 5¼" high

Materials
Modacrylic three-ply carpet yarn or a similar substitute, 2 ounces of white and 1½ ounces of color

aluminum crochet hook size E or size that will give an acceptable gauge.

Gauge
6 stitches = 1 inch, 4½ rows = 1 inch.

Medium Basket

Size
5¼" diameter by 7½" high

Materials
Modacrylic three-ply carpet yarn or a similar substitute, 4 ounces of white and 3 ounces of color;

aluminum crochet hook size E or size that will give an acceptable gauge.

Gauge
6 stitches = 1 inch, 4½ rows = 1 inch.

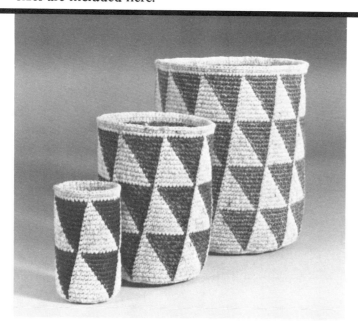

Photo 28. Small, medium and large baskets worked from the same pattern.

Large Basket

Size
8¼" diameter by 10" high

Materials
Modacrylic three-ply carpet yarn or a similar substitute, 8 ounces of white and 7 ounces of color;

aluminum crochet hook size E or size that will give an acceptable gauge.

Gauge
6 stitches = 1 inch, 4½ rows = 1 inch.

Round 1: Starting with the white yarn, make a slip knot, then chain 4 stitches. Join the ends together to form a ring by working a slip stitch into the first chain stitch.

Round 2: Single crochet 6 stitches loosely into the ring. The basket should have a total of 6 stitches when you finish this round. Slip a safety pin into the last stitch if you want to keep track of where each round ends. Remove the safety pin from the last stitch as you come to it again and slip it into the new last stitch.

Round 3: Start to carry the color yarn. Increase in every stitch to 12 stitches.

Round 4: Increase in every stitch to 24 stitches.

Round 5: Increase in every second stitch to 36 stitches.

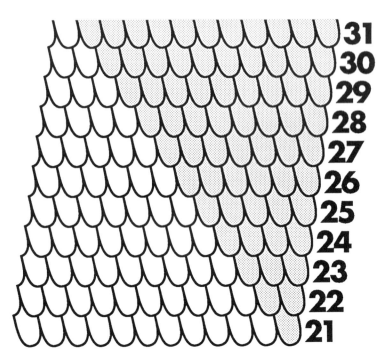

Graph 6.

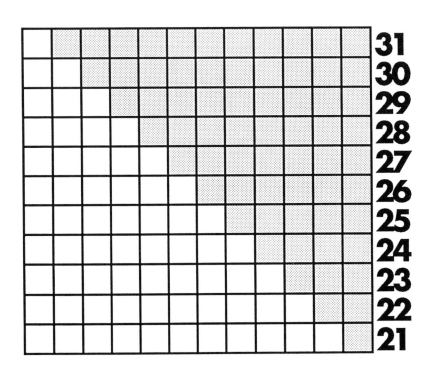

Graph 6S.

Round 6: Single crochet one round without any increases.

Round 7: Increase in every third stitch. The basket should have 48 stitches when you finish this round.

If you are crocheting the Small Basket, stop the base here and go on to Round 21.

Round 8: Single crochet one round without any increases.

72

Photo 29. Face of the triangular motif basket.

Round 9: Increase in every fourth stitch to 60 stitches.

Round 10: Increase in every fifth stitch to 72 stitches.

Round 11: Single crochet one round without any increases.

Round 12: Increase in every sixth stitch to 84 stitches.

Round 13: Increase in every seventh stitch. The basket should have 96 stitches when you finish this round.

If you are crocheting the Medium Basket, stop the base here and go on to Round 21.

Round 14: Increase in every eighth stitch to 108 stitches.

Round 15: Single crochet one round without any increases.

Round 16: Increase in every ninth stitch to 120 stitches.

Round 17: Increase in every tenth stitch to 132 stitches.

Round 18: Single crochet one round without any increases.

Round 19: Increase in every eleventh stitch to 144 stitches.

Round 20: Single crochet one round without any increases.

Begin Sides

Round 21: Start the triangular motif as follows: tapestry crochet 1 color, 11 white stitches. Repeat this sequence around. The number of stitches will now remain constant from round to round.

Round 22: Tapestry crochet 2 color, 10 white stitches. Repeat around.

Round 23: Tapestry crochet 3 color, 9 white stitches. Repeat around.

Round 24: Tapestry crochet 4 color, 8 white stitches. Repeat around.

Round 25: Tapestry crochet 5 color, 7 white stitches. Repeat around.

Round 26: Tapestry crochet 6 color, 6 white stitches. Repeat around.

Photo 30. Reverse side of the triangular motif basket.

73

Round 27: Tapestry crochet 7 color, 5 white stitches. Repeat around.

Round 28: Tapestry crochet 8 color, 4 white stitches. Repeat around.

Round 29: Tapestry crochet 9 color, 3 white stitches. Repeat around.

Round 30: Tapestry crochet 10 color, 2 white stitches. Repeat around.

Round 31: Tapestry crochet 11 color, 1 white stitches. Repeat around.

Repeat rounds 21 through 31 as many times as you wish.

Finishing

To finish the basket, single crochet 2 rows of white, continuously carrying the color yarn until the last 3 stitches. *(Photo 31.)* Cut the color yarn flush. Single crochet the last 3 white stitches. Finish off. Work in the end. Block the basket.

Photo 31. Detail, border rounds.

These attractive shoulder bags are actually baskets with a unique and functional strap. *Photo 32* and *Plate 8* illustrate how the looped strap works. The motif in *Graph 7* is based on a Guatemalan design. Both bags are worked from the instructions below.

Cylindrical Shoulder Bags

Tall Shoulder Bag

Size
7" diameter by 13" high (not including strap)

Materials
Modacrylic three-ply carpet yarn or a similar substitute, 4 ounces of white, 12 ounces of color;

aluminum crochet hook size D or size that will give an acceptable gauge.

Gauge
6 stitches = 1 inch, 4½ rows = 1 inch.

Photo 32. Two cylindrical shoulder bags with horse motif.

Short Shoulder Bag

Size
7" diameter by 9½" high (not including strap)

Materials
Wool blend carpet yarn or a similar substitute, 4 ounces of white and 12 ounces of color;

aluminum crochet hook size D or the size that will give an acceptable gauge.

Gauge
6 stitches = 1 inch 4½ rows = 1 inch

Round 1: Starting with the color yarn, make a slip knot, then chain 4 stitches. Join the ends together to form a ring by working a slip stitch into the first chain stitch.

Round 2: Single crochet 6 stitches into the ring loosely. The shoulder bag should have a total of 6 stitches when you finish this round. Slip a safety pin into the last stitch if you want to keep track of where each round ends. Remove the safety pin from the last stitch as you come to it again and slip it into the new last stitch.

Round 3: Start to carry the white yarn. Increase in every stitch. There will be 12 stitches when you finish this round.

Round 4: Increase in every stitch to 24 stitches.

Round 5: Increase in every second stitch to 36 stitches.

Round 6: Increase in every third stitch to 48 stitches.

Round 7: Single crochet one round without any increases.

Round 8: Increase in every fourth stitch to 60 stitches.

Round 9: Increase in every fifth stitch to 72 stitches.

Round 10: Single crochet one round without any increases.

Round 11: Increase in every sixth stitch to 84 stitches. Don't worry if the base isn't flat; it will flatten out during blocking.

Round 12: Increase in every seventh stitch to 96 stitches.

Round 13: Single crochet one round without any increases.

Round 14: Increase in every eighth stitch to 108 stitches.

Graph 7.

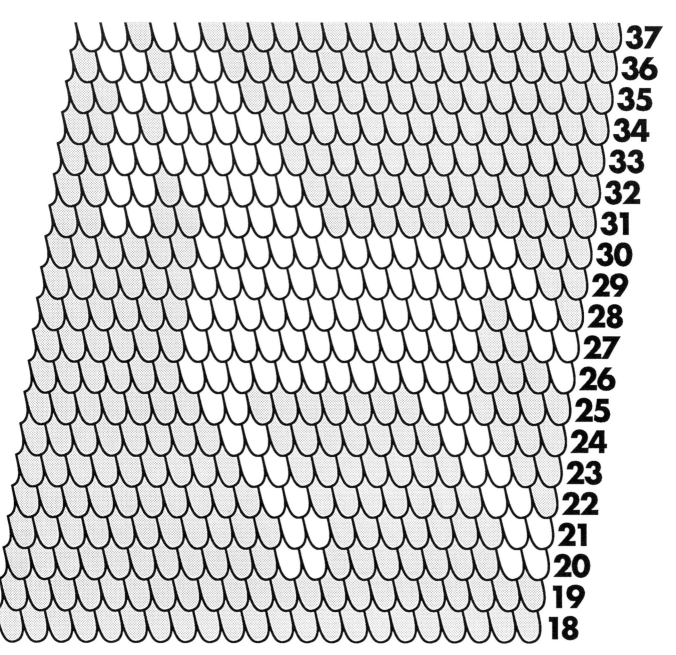

Round 15: Increase in every ninth stitch to 120 stitches.

Round 16: Increase in every tenth stitch to 132 stitches.

Begin Sides

Round 17: Single crochet one round without any increases. Each round will have 132 stitches from now on.

Rounds 18 and 19: Single crochet one plain round without any increases or color changes.

Round 20: Start the horse motif as follows *(Graph 7S)* tapestry crochet 2 white, 7 color, 2 white, 11 color stitches. Repeat this sequence 5 more times.

Round 21: Tapestry crochet 2 white, 7 color, 2 white, 11 color stitches. Repeat this sequence 5 more times.

Graph 7S.

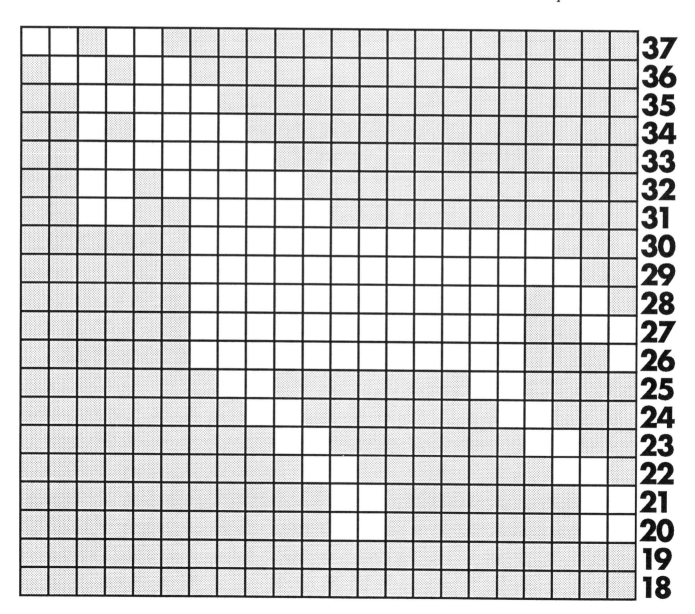

37
36
35
34
33
32
31
30
29
28
27
26
25
24
23
22
21
20
19
18

Photo 33. Detail, face of the horse motif shoulder bag.

Photo 34. Detail, reverse side of the horse motif shoulder bag.

Round 22: Tapestry crochet 1 color, 2 white, 7 color, 2 white, 10 color stitches. Repeat this sequence 5 more times.

Round 23: Tapestry crochet 2 color, 2 white, 7 color, 2 white, 9 color stitches. Repeat around.

Round 24: Tapestry crochet 3 color, 2 white, 7 color, 2 white, 8 color stitches. Repeat around

Round 25: Tapestry crochet 4 color, 2 white, 7 color, 2 white, 7 color stitches. Repeat around.

Round 26: Tapestry crochet 1 white, 3 color, 12 white, 6 color stitches. Repeat around.

Round 27: Tapestry crochet 2 white, 2 color, 12 white, 6 color stitches. Repeat around.

Round 28: Tapestry crochet 1 color, 2 white, 1 color, 12 white, 6 color stitches. Repeat around.

Round 29: Tapestry crochet 2 color, 14 white, 6 color stitches. Repeat around.

Round 30: Tapestry crochet 3 color, 13 white, 6 color stitches. Repeat around.

Round 31: Tapestry crochet 11 color, 5 white, 2 color, 2 white, 2 color stitches. Repeat around.

Round 32: Tapestry crochet 12 color, 5 white, 1 color, 2 white, 2 color stitches. Repeat around.

Round 33: Tapestry crochet 13 color, 7 white, 2 color stitches. Repeat around.

Round 34: Tapestry crochet 14 color, 4 white, 1 color, 1 white, 2 color stitches. Repeat around.

Round 35: Tapestry crochet 15 color, 5 white, 2 color stitches. Repeat around.

Round 36: Tapestry crochet 16 color, 2 white, 1 color, 2 white, 1 color stitch. Repeat around.

Round 37: Tapestry crochet 17 color, 2 white, 1 color, 2 white stitches. Repeat around.

Repeat rounds 18 through 37 two more times for the tall bag, or one more time for the short bag.

Looped Shoulder Strap

A: Continuing around the bag, single crochet 4 color stitches. Cut the white yarn flush. Chain 10 in color, skip 10 stitches of the previous row, start to carry the white yarn again (slit formed); single crochet 60 stitches. Chain 130 color stitches, insert the hook into the next stitch (the chain will form a large loop) and finish the round by single crocheting 58 more stitches. *(Photo 35 and figure 43.)*

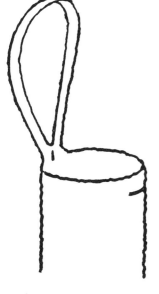

43. Shoulder strap loop and slot.

Photo 35. Detail, looped shoulder strap

Cylindrical Shoulder Bag
continued

B, C, D, and E: Single crochet 262 stitches around bag and strap with the color yarn, still carrying the white yarn.

F: Single crochet 259 stitches with the color yarn. Cut the white yarn flush. Single crochet the last three color stitches. Finish off.

Finishing

Work in the end. Block the shoulder bag and strap. Pull the strap through the 10-stitch loop to close the bag. *(figure 44.)*

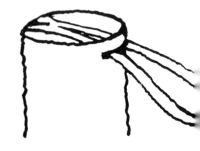

44. Bag closure.

The beautiful shape of this basket is achieved by increasing and decreasing the stitches that make up the sides. Sides are patterned with the design in Graph 7. A crocheted lid tops this unusual project. Review increasing, decreasing and shaping, page 28. Once you have mastered the shaping technique, you will be able to create your own unique basket shapes

Shaped Basket with Lid

Basket

Size
10" wide by 7½" tall
Lid 5¼" wide
by 1¼" tall

Materials
Heavy 100% Polypropylene Rug Yarn or a similar substitute, 3 1/5 ounces of white and 9 3/5 ounces of color;

aluminum crochet hook size C or the size that will give an acceptable gauge.

Gauge
6½ stitches = 1 inch,
6 rows = 1 inch.

Photo 36. Shaped basket with separately-crocheted lid.

Basket

Round 1: Starting with the color yarn, make a slip knot, then chain 4 stitches. Join the ends together to form a ring by working a slip knot into the first chain stitch.

Round 2: Single crochet 6 stitches loosely into the ring. The base should have a total of 6 stitches when you finish this round. Slip a safety pin into the last stitch if you want to keep track of where each round ends. Remove the safety pin from the last stitch as you come around to it again and then slip it into the last stitch of the round that you have just finished.

Round 3: Start to carry the white yarn. Increase in every stitch. The base should have 12 stitches when you finish this round.

Round 4: Increase in every stitch to 24 stitches.

Round 5: Increase in every second stitch to 36 stitches.

Round 6: Increase in every third stitch to 48 stitches.

Round 7: Single crochet one round without any increases.

Round 8: Increase in every fourth stitch to 60 stitches.

Round 9: Increase in every fifth stitch to 72 stitches.

Round 10: Single crochet one round without any increases.

Round 11: Increase in every sixth stitch to 84 stitches. Do not worry if the base is not flat; it will flatten after it is blocked.

Round 12: Increase in every seventh stitch to 96 stitches.

Round 13: Single crochet one round without any increases.

Round 14: Increase in every eighth stitch to 108 stitches.

Round 15: Increase in every ninth stitch to 120 stitches.

Round 16: Increase in every tenth stitch to 132 stitches.

Begin Sides

Rounds 17 through 24: Single crochet one round without any increases. The basket should still have 132 stitches.

Round 25: Increase in every eleventh stitch to 144 stitches.

Rounds 26 and 27: Single crochet one round without any increases.

Round 28: Increase in every twelfth stitch to 156 stitches.

Round 29: Single crochet one round without any increases.

Round 30: Increase in every thirteenth stitch to 168 stitches.

Round 31: Single crochet one round without any increases.

Round 32: Increase in every fourteenth stitch to 180 stitches.

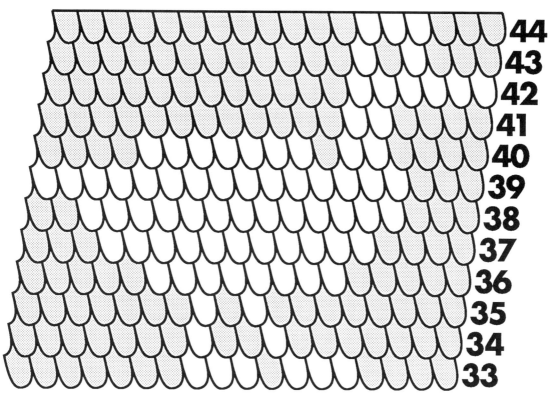

Graph 8.

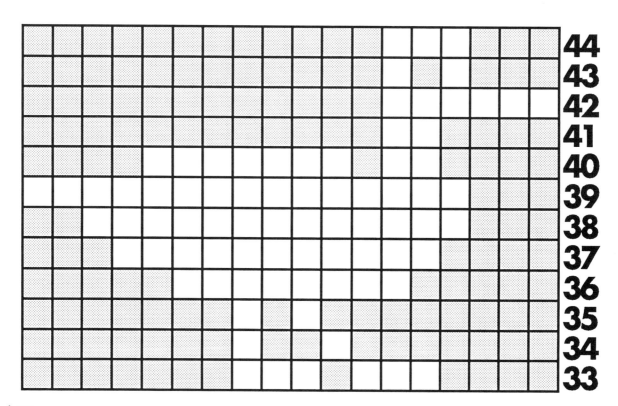

Graph 8S.

Round 33: Start the duck motif *(Graph 8S)*. There are no increases in this section, so each round will have 180 stitches. Tapestry crochet 4 color, 3 white, 1 color, 3 white; 7 color stitches. Repeat this sequence 9 more times.

Round 34: Tapestry crochet 7 color, 1 white, 2 color, 1 white, 7 color stitches. Repeat this sequence 9 more times.

Round 35: Tapestry crochet 8 color, 1 white, 1 color, 1 white, 7 color stitches. Repeat this sequence 9 more times.

Round 36: Tapestry crochet 5 color, 8 white, 5 color stitches. Repeat around.

Round 37: Tapestry crochet 4 color, 11 white, 3 color stitches. Repeat around.

Round 38: Tapestry crochet 3 color, 13 white, 2 color stitches. Repeat around.

Round 39: Tapestry crochet 3 color, 15 white stitches. Repeat around.

Round 40: Tapestry crochet 4 color, 2 white, 1 color, 7 white, 4 color stitches. Repeat around.

Round 41: Tapestry crochet 4 color, 2 white, 12 color stitches. Repeat around.

Round 42: Tapestry crochet 6 white, 12 color stitches. Repeat around.

Round 43: Tapestry crochet 3 color, 1 white, 1 color, 1 white, 12 color stitches. Repeat around.

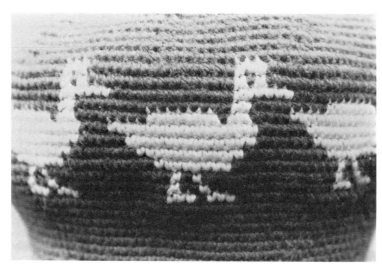

Photo 37. Detail of the shaped basket with duck motif.

Round 44: Tapestry crochet 3 color, 3 white, 12 color stitches. Repeat around.

Round 45: Although the duck motif is finished, continue to carry the white yarn through the remaining rows. With the color yarn, decrease in every fourteenth stitch to 168 stitches.

Round 46: Single crochet one round without any decreases.

Round 47: Decrease in every thirteenth stitch to 156 stitches.

Round 48: Single crochet one round without any decreases.

Round 49: Decrease in every twelfth stitch to 144 stitches.

Round 50: Single crochet one round without any decreases.

Round 51: Decrease in every eleventh stitch to 132 stitches.

Round 52: Single crochet one round without any decreases.

Round 53: Decrease in every tenth stitch to 120 stitches.

Round 54: Single crochet one round without any decreases.

Round 55: Decrease in every ninth stitch to 108 stitches.

Round 56: Single crochet one round without any decreases.

Round 57: Decrease in every eighth stitch to 96 stitches.

Round 58: Single crochet one round without any decreases.

Round 59: Decrease in every seventh stitch to 84 stitches.

Rounds 60 through 63: Single crochet one round without any decreases. The basket should still have 84 stitches.

Final Round

Round 64: Single crochet one round without any decreases. Continue to carry the white yarn until the last three stitches. Cut the white yarn flush, then single crochet the last three stitches with color. Finish off. Work in the end.

Lid

Round 1: Starting with the white yarn, make a slip knot, then chain 4 stitches. Join the ends together to form a ring by working a slip knot into the first chain stitch.

Round 2: Single crochet 6 stitches into the ring loosely. The lid should have a total of 6 stitches when you finish this round. Use a safety pin as before to keep track of rows if you wish.

Round 3: Start to carry the color yarn. Increase in every stitch to 12 stitches.

Round 4: Increase in every stitch to 24 stitches.

Round 5: Increase in every second stitch to 36 stitches.

Round 6: Increase in every third stitch to 48 stitches.

Round 7: Single crochet one round without any increases.

Round 8: Increase in every fourth stitch to 60 stitches.

Round 9: Increase in every fifth stitch to 72 stitches.

Round 10: Single crochet one round without any increases.

Round 11: Increase in every sixth stitch to 84 stitches. Do not worry if the lid is not flat. It will flatten out after it has been blocked.

Round 12: Increase in every seventh stitch to 96 stitches.

Rounds 13 through 19: Single crochet one round without any increases. The lid will have 96 stitches from now on.

Round 20: Single crochet one round without any increases. Continue to carry the color yarn until the last three stitches. Cut the color yarn flush, then single crochet the last three stitches with white.

Finish off. Work in the end. Block the basket and lid.

Photo 38. Detail, basket lid.

7. Flat Tapestry Crochet Projects

Flat, rectangular pieces can be made by changing the stitch used at the end of a row to work back across the piece. In the two wall hanging projects that follow, either the Reverse Single Crochet *(Method A)*, or the Alternate-Row Switch-Hands Single Crochet *(Method B)* can be used to work back-and-forth. See *Plates 11* and *15*. Whichever method you choose, use it *consistently* throughout the piece. At first the unusual working method may feel awkward, however the result is well worth the initial extra effort.

Arrows at the left edge of the graphs indicate the working direction of the stitches for that row. Two yarns are carried throughout the wall hanging, allowing for the working of more complex motifs.

Wall Hanging

Wall Hanging

Size
14½" wide by
12½" high

Materials
100% Dacron Rug Yarn, or a similar substitute, 4½ ounces of light blue, 1¼ ounces of red, and 1½ ounces of beige;

two 15" long ½" diameter dowels;

aluminum crochet hook size C or the size that will give an acceptable gauge.

Gauge
7 stitches = 1 inch, 5½ rows = 1 inch.

Photo 39. "Someday..." people/heart motif wall hanging.

Row 1: Starting with the light blue yarn, make a slip knot, then chain 97 stitches. Increase or decrease in multiples of 16 at this point to make a wider or narrower wall hanging.

Row 2: Starting with the second chain, single crochet 96 stitches.

Row 3: Start to carry the red and beige yarns. Chain 1 with blue. In this row you need to choose flat-work method A or B to work each odd-numbered row. Work across with blue.

Graph 9.(above) Detail of crochet graph for "Someday..."

Graph 9S. (opposite page) Working graph for "Someday..." Arrows indicate working direction for each row.

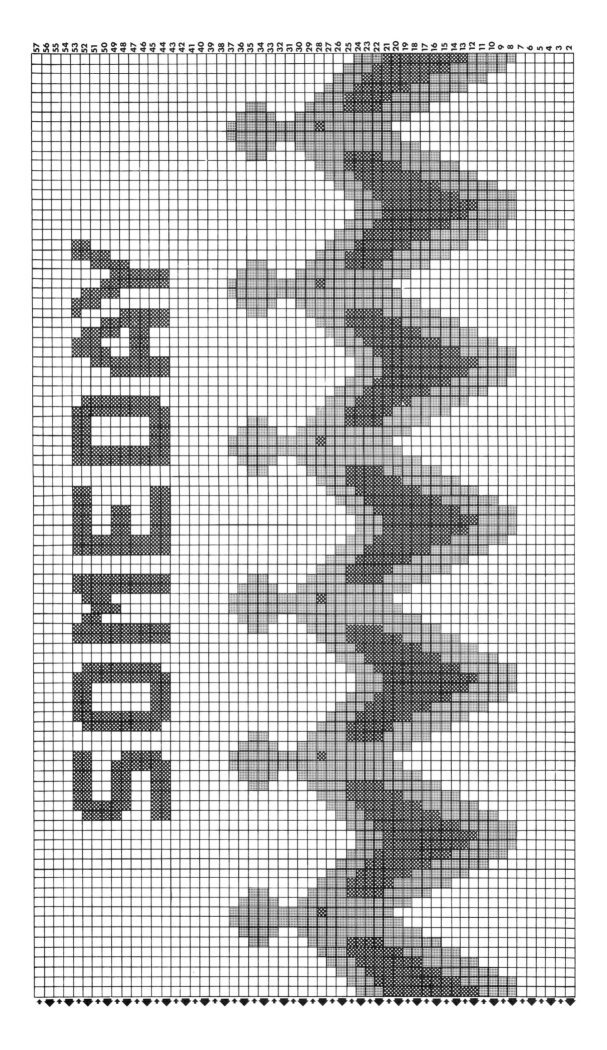

Photo 40. Face of the "Someday..." wall hanging.

Photo 41. Reverse side of the "Someday..." wall hanging

Row 4: Chain 1, then single crochet across with blue.

Row 5: Chain 1, then work across with blue with Method A or B.

Row 6: Chain 1, single crochet across with blue.

Row 7: Chain 1, work across with blue with Method A or B. Do not worry if the piece curls. When it is finished and blocked it will be flat.

Row 8: Chain 1 with beige, then repeat the following sequence six times: tapestry crochet 1 beige, 13 blue, and then 2 beige stitches.

Row 9: Chain 1 with beige. In order to work the tapestry crochet stitch on this, and on all the other odd-numbered rows, using Method A or B repeat the following sequence six times: tapestry crochet 2 beige, 12 blue, 2 beige stitches.

Row 10: Chain 1 with beige, then repeat the following sequence six times: tapestry crochet 2 beige, 11 blue, 3 beige stitches.

Row 11: Chain 1 with beige, then using either Method A or B, repeat the following sequence six times: tapestry crochet 3 beige, 10 blue, 3 beige stitches.

Row 12: Chain 1 with beige, then repeat across: tapestry crochet 3 beige, 9 blue, 3 beige, 1 red stitch.

Row 13: Chain 1 with red, then repeat across: tapestry crochet 1 red, 3 beige, 8 blue, 3 beige, 1 red stitch.

Row 14: Chain 1 with red, then repeat across: tapestry crochet 1 red, 3 beige, 7 blue, 3 beige, 2 red stitches.

90

Row 15: Chain 1 with red, then repeat across: tapestry crochet 2 red, 3 beige, 6 blue, 3 beige, 2 red stitches.

Row 16: Chain 1 with red, then repeat across: tapestry crochet 2 red, 3 beige, 5 blue, 3 beige, 3 red stitches.

Row 17: Chain 1 with red, then repeat across: tapestry crochet 3 red, 3 beige, 4 blue, 3 beige, 3 red stitches.

Row 18: Chain 1 with red, then repeat across: tapestry crochet 3 red, 3 beige, 3 blue, 3 beige, 4 red stitches.

Row 19: Chain 1 with red, then repeat across: tapestry crochet 4 red, 3 beige, 2 blue, 3 beige, 4 red stitches.

Row 20: Chain 1 with red, then repeat across: tapestry crochet 4 red, 3 beige, 1 blue, 3 beige, 5 red stitches.

Row 21: Chain 1 with red, then repeat across: tapestry crochet 5 red, 6 beige, 5 red stitches.

Row 22: Chain 1 with beige, then repeat across: tapestry crochet 1 beige, 5 red, 4 beige, 5 red, 1 beige stitch.

Row 23: Chain 1 with beige, then repeat across: tapestry crochet 2 beige, 4 red, 4 beige, 4 red, 2 beige stitches.

Row 24: Chain 1 with beige, then repeat across: tapestry crochet 3 beige, 3 red, 4 beige, 3 red, 3 beige stitches.

Row 25: Chain 1 with blue, then repeat across: tapestry crochet 1 blue, 3 beige, 2 red, 4 beige, 2 red, 3 beige, 1 blue stitch.

Row 26: Chain 1 with blue, then repeat across: tapestry crochet 2 blue, 12 beige, 2 blue stitches.

Row 27: Chain 1 with blue, then repeat across: tapestry crochet 3 blue, 10 beige, 3 blue stitches.

Row 28: Chain 1 with blue, then repeat across: tapestry crochet 4 blue, 3 beige, 1 red, 4 beige, 4 blue stitches.

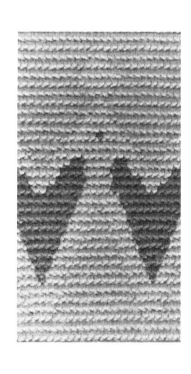

Photo 42. Close detail, front of wall hanging.

Photo 43. Close detail, reverse side of wall hanging.

Row 29: Chain 1 with blue, then repeat across: tapestry crochet 5 blue, 6 beige, 5 blue stitches.

Row 30: Chain 1 with blue, then repeat across: tapestry crochet 6 blue, 4 beige, 6 blue stitches.

Rows 31 and 32: Chain 1 with blue, then repeat across: tapestry crochet 7 blue, 2 beige, 7 blue stitches.

Row 33: Chain 1 with blue, then repeat across: tapestry crochet 6 blue, 4 beige, 6 blue stitches.

Rows 34 and 35: Chain 1 with blue, then repeat across: tapestry crochet 5 blue, 6 beige, 5 blue stitches.

Row 36: Chain 1 with blue, then repeat across: tapestry crochet 6 blue, 4 beige, 6 blue stitches.

Row 37: Chain 1 with blue, then repeat across: tapestry crochet 7 blue, 2 beige, 7 blue stitches.

Rows 38 through 43: Chain 1, then single crochet across with blue.

Begin letters

Row 44: Chain 1 with blue. In this row you will start to crochet the letters as follows: tapestry crochet 22 blue, 2 red, 2 blue, 2 red, 3 blue, 2 red, 3 blue, 6 red, 2 blue, 7 red, 2 blue, 2 red, 3 blue, 2 red, 3 blue, 5 red, 4 blue, 6 red, 18 blue stitches.

Row 45: Chain 1 with blue, tapestry crochet 18 blue, 7 red, 2 blue, 7 red, 2 blue, 2 red, 3 blue, 2 red, 2 blue, 7 red, 2 blue, 7 red, 2 blue, 2 red, 3 blue, 2 red, 2 blue, 2 red, 22 blue stitches.

Row 46: Chain 1 with blue, tapestry crochet 22 blue, 2 red, 2 blue, 7 red, 2 blue, 2 red, 3 blue, 2 red, 7 blue, 2 red, 2 blue, 2 red, 3 blue, 2 red, 2 blue, 2 red, 3 blue, 2 red, 2 blue, 2 red, 23 blue stitches.

Row 47: Chain 1 with blue, tapestry crochet 23 blue, 2 red, 2 blue, 2 red, 3 blue, 2 red, 2 blue, 2 red, 3 blue, 2 red, 2 blue, 2 red, 7 blue, 2 red, 3 blue, 2 red, 2 blue, 7 red, 2 blue, 2 red, 22 blue stitches.

Row 48: Chain 1 with blue, tapestry crochet 21 blue, 3 red, 2 blue, 2 red, 3 blue, 2 red, 2 blue, 2 red, 3 blue, 2 red, 4 blue, 5 red, 2 blue, 2 red, 3 blue, 2 red, 2 blue, 2 red, 3 blue, 2 red, 2 blue, 6 red, 19 blue stitches.

Row 49: Chain 1 with blue, tapestry crochet 18 blue, 6 red, 3 blue, 2 red, 3 blue, 2 red, 2 blue, 2 red, 1 blue, 1 red, 1 blue, 2 red, 2 blue, 5 red, 4 blue, 2 red, 3 blue, 2 red, 2 blue, 2 red, 2 blue, 2 red, 2 blue, 4 red, 21 blue stitches.

Row 50: Chain 1 with blue, tapestry crochet 20 blue, 2 red, 1 blue, 2 red, 2 blue, 2 red, 1 blue, 2 red, 3 blue, 2 red, 3 blue, 2 red, 7 blue, 2 red, 2 blue, 4 red, 1 blue, 2 red, 2 blue, 2 red, 3 blue, 2 red, 7 blue, 2 red, 18 blue stitches.

Row 51: Chain 1 with blue, tapestry crochet 18 blue, 2 red, 7 blue, 2 red, 3 blue, 2 red, 2 blue, 7 red, 2 blue, 2 red, 7 blue, 2 red, 3 blue, 2 red, 3 blue, 4 red, 2 blue, 2 red, 2 blue, 2 red, 20 blue stitches.

Row 52: Chain 1 with blue, tapestry crochet 19 blue, 2 red, 3 blue, 2 red, 2 blue, 3 red, 4 blue, 7 red, 2 blue, 7 red, 2 blue, 3 red, 1 blue, 3 red, 2 blue, 7 red, 2 blue, 7 red, 18 blue stitches.

Row 53: Chain 1 with blue, tapestry crochet 19 blue, 6 red, 3 blue, 5 red, 3 blue, 2 red, 3 blue, 2 red, 2 blue, 7 red, 2 blue, 6 red, 5 blue, 2 red, 2 blue, 2 red, 4 blue, 2 red, 19 blue stitches.

Rows 54 through 57: Chain 1, single crochet across with blue.

Photo 44. Detail, "I Still Have a Dream..." wall hanging with figures in several colors, based on "Someday..." graph. Full view is shown in Plate 18.

93

Border   *A:* Single crochet a blue border around the four sides clockwise, carrying the beige and red yarns.

B: Single crochet the border across the top and one side; cut the red and beige yarns flush. To crochet the bottom loops repeat the following sequence 49 times: Chain 9, single crochet 2 stitches. Start to carry the beige and red yarns while single crocheting up the final side, then cut the beige and red yarns flush.

C: Crochet the top loops by repeating the following sequence 49 times: Chain 9, single crochet 2 stitches. At the end of this row finish off. Work in the end.

Finishing   If part of the hanging is much wider or lumpy, turn it over. Using a small crochet hook, pull some of the carried yarns from the back until the hanging flattens out or gets narrower. The loops formed from pulling the carried yarns can be cut flush as long as they are secured on both sides.

Block the wall hanging, then insert the dowels through the loops, one in each end of the hanging.

Photo 45. Detail of "Someday" border.

A photographic image is the unique feature of this flat tapestry crochet project. Two colors are carried throughout the design, shown in *Graph 10S.* Arrows at the left edge of the graph indicate working direction for each row. See *Plate 11.*

A slide projector or an opaque projector can be used to project an image onto #2 graph paper. The image can be traced on the graph paper, and the appropriate areas colored in. Finally, the design is transferred from #2 graph paper onto square-ruled graph paper to follow while crocheting. *Photo 47* is the original photograph that was projected to make *Graph 10.*

To make a tapestry with more detail or sharper images, the image can be projected onto a larger graph, made up of many more stitches. Several copies of graph paper #2 may be taped together to form a large sheet. The height of the stitch can distort the image, so a sample piece should be crocheted to determine the rows-per-inch measurement needed to reproduce an exact image.

Wall Hanging

Size
15" wide by
12¼" high

Materials
Mill end 100% wool
3-ply carpet yarn,
or a similar substitute, 10
ounces of white,
3 ounces of beige, and
3 ounces of brown;

one 16" long,
½" diameter dowel;

aluminum crochet hook
size E
or the size that will give
an acceptable gauge.

Gauge
4½ stitches = 1 inch,
3½ rows = 1 inch.

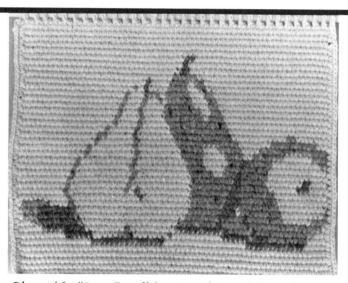

Photo 46. "Pears" wall hanging designed from the photographic image in Photo 47 (next page).

Row 1: Starting with the white yarn, make a slip knot, then chain 66 stitches.

Row 2: Starting with the second chain, single crochet 65 stitches.

Row 3: Start to carry the beige and brown yarns. Chain 1 with white. In this row you need to choose Method A or B to work on each odd-numbered row.

Row 4: Chain 1 with white. Single crochet across with white.

Row 5: Chain 1 with white; work across in Method A or B with white.

Row 6: Chain 1 with white; single crochet across with white.

Row 7: Start the motif on this row. Chain 1 with white. In order to tapestry crochet on this, and on all other odd-numbered rows with Method A or B, tapestry crochet 15 white, 15 brown, 17 white, 13 brown, 5 white stitches.

Row 8: Chain 1 with white, tapestry crochet 4 white, 9 beige, 10 brown, 10 white, 1 beige, 7 white, 1 brown, 2 beige, 5 white, 6 brown, 10 white stitches.

Row 9: Chain 1 with white, then using either Method A or B: tapestry crochet 5 white, 1 beige, 8 brown, 8 white, 1 beige, 9 white, 1 beige, 10 brown, 5 beige, 1 brown, 13 beige; end with 3 white stitches.

Row 10: Chain 1 with white, tapestry crochet 1 white, 16 beige, 1 brown, 5 beige, 1 brown, 8 beige, 19 white, 1 beige, 8 brown, 2 beige, 3 white stitches.

Row 11: Chain 1 with white; With Method A or B, tapestry crochet 1 white, 3 beige, 8 brown, 1 beige, 21 white, 7 beige, 2 brown, 3 beige, 1 brown, 8 beige, 6 white, 4 beige stitches.

Row 12: Chain 1 with beige, tapestry crochet 1 beige, 9 white, 10 beige, 3 brown, 7 beige, 22 white, 1 beige, 7 brown, 4 beige, 1 white stitch.

Photo 47. This black and white photograph was projected onto the #2 graph paper to make the wallhanging design.

Photo 48. Detail, face of pear motif wall hanging.

Photo 49. Detail, reverse of the pear motif wall hanging.

Row 13: Chain 1 with white, tapestry crochet 1 white, 6 beige, 4 white, 1 beige, 23 white, 7 beige, 3 brown, 9 beige, 10 white, 1 beige stitch.

Row 14: Chain 1 with white, tapestry crochet 11 white, 8 beige, 3 brown, 8 beige, 9 white, 1 brown, 13 white, 1 beige, 11 white stitches.

Row 15: Chain 1 with white, tapestry crochet 10 white, 1 beige, 11 white, 1 beige, 1 white, 1 brown, 10 white, 8 beige, 2 brown, 8 beige, 1 white, 1 beige stitch.

Row 16: Chain 1 with white, tapestry crochet 4 white, 3 brown, 6 white, 6 beige, 2 brown, 9 beige, 11 white, 1 beige, 11 white, 1 beige, 11 white stitches.

Row 17: Chain 1 with white, tapestry crochet 11 white, 1 beige, 11 white, 1 beige, 11 white, 9 beige, 1 brown, 6 beige, 8 white, 2 brown, 3 white, 1 beige stitch.

Row 18: Chain 1 with white, tapestry crochet 13 white, 6 beige, 1 brown, 3 beige, 2 white, 5 beige, 10 white, 1 beige, 11 white, 1 beige, 12 white stitches.

Row 19: Chain 1 with white, tapestry crochet 12 white, 1 beige, 10 whie, 1 beige, 10 white, 4 beige, 4 white, 3 beige, 1 brown, 6 beige, 12 white, 1 beige stitch.

Row 20: Chain 1 with beige, tapestry crochet 2 beige, 10 white, 6 beige, 1 white, 3 beige, 5 white, 4 beige, 9 white, 1 beige, 10 white, 1 beige, 13 white stitches.

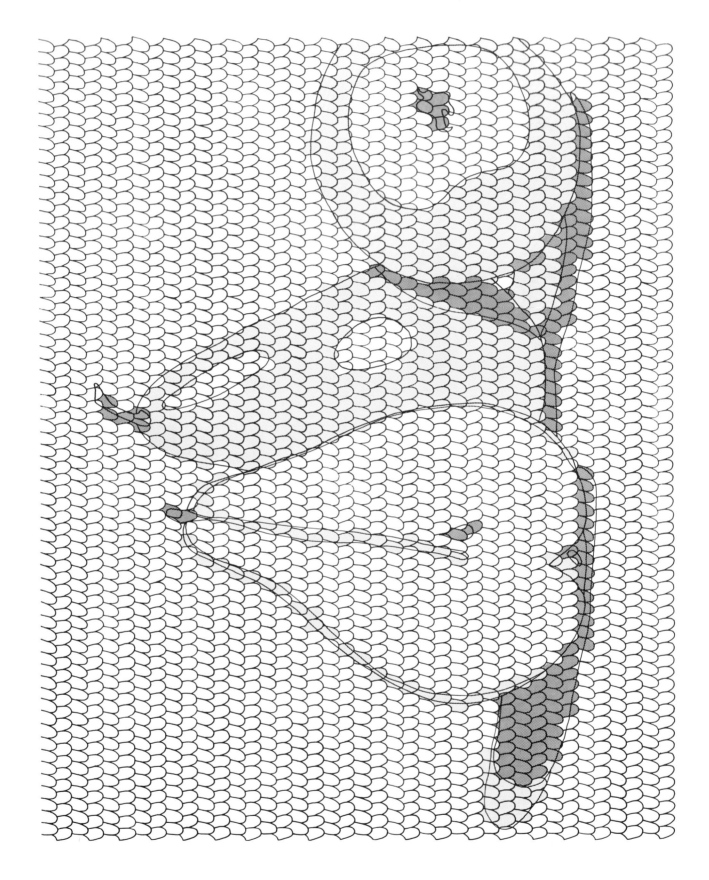

Graph 10. (above).

Graph 10S. (opposite page) Arrows at left edge indicate working direction for each row.

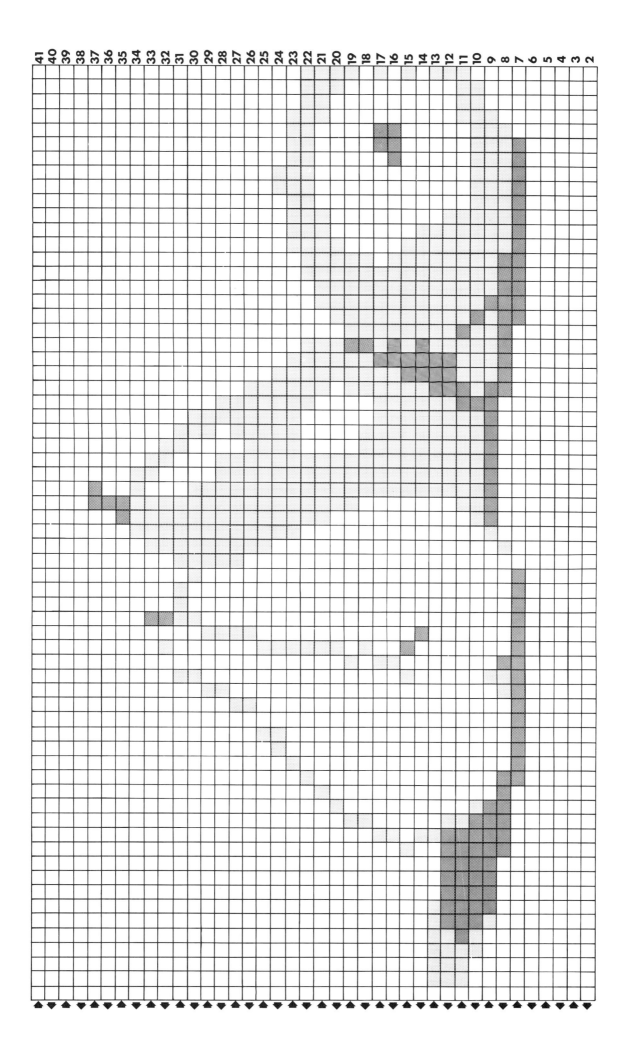

Row 21: Chain 1 with white, tapestry crochet
14 white, 1 beige, 9 white, 1 beige, 8 white,
5 beige, 4 white, 4 beige, 2 white, 7 beige,
6 white, 4 beige stitches.

Row 22: Chain 1 with beige, tapestry crochet
15 beige, 4 white, 5 beige, 3 white, 5 beige, 8 white,
1 beige, 8 white, 1 beige, 15 white stitches.

Row 23: Chain 1 with white, tapestry crochet
16 white, 1 beige, 7 white, 1 beige, 7 white, 13 beige,
7 white, 10 beige, 3 white stitches.

Row 24: Chain 1 with white, tapestry crochet
7 white, 2 beige, 12 white, 12 beige, 7 white, 1 beige,
5 white, 2 beige, 17 white stitches.

Row 25: Chain 1 with white, tapestry crochet
18 white, 1 beige, 5 white, 1 beige, 6 white, 12 beige,
22 white stitches.

Row 26: Chain 1 with white, tapestry crochet
2 white, 12 beige, 5 white, 1 beige, 4 white, 1 beige,
20 white stitches.

Row 27: Chain 1 with white, tapestry crochet
20 white, 1 beige, 4 white, 1 beige, 4 white, 8 beige,
1 white, 3 beige, 23 white stitches.

Row 28: Chain 1 with white, tapestry crochet
23 white, 2 beige, 2 white, 8 beige, 4 white, 1 beige,
3 white, 1 beige, 21 white stitches.

Row 29: Chain 1 with white, tapestry crochet
21 white, 1 beige, 3 white, 1 beige, 4 white, 6 beige,
3 white, 2 beige, 24 white stitches.

Row 30: Chain 1 with white, tapestry crochet
24 white, 2 beige, 3 white, 7 beige, 2 white, 1 beige,
3 white, 1 beige, 22 white stitches.

Row 31: Chain 1 with white, tapestry crochet
22 white, 1 beige, 3 white, 3 beige, 1 white,
5 beige, 3 white, 2 beige, 25 white stitches.

*Photo 50. Close detail,
face of wall hanging.*

*Photo 51. Close detail,
reverse side of wall
hanging.*

Row 32: Chain 1 with white, tapestry crochet 26 white, 2 beige, 2 white, 4 beige, 4 white, 1 brown, 1 white, 1 beige, 24 white stitches.

Row 33: Chain 1 with white, tapestry crochet 26 white, 1 brown, 4 white, 4 beige, 1 white, 2 beige, 27 white stitches.

Row 34: Chain 1 with white, tapestry crochet 28 white, 5 beige, 32 white stitches.

Row 35: Chain 1 with white, tapestry crochet 33 white, 2 brown, 30 white stitches.

Row 36: Chain 1 with white, tapestry crochet 30 white, 1 brown, 34 white stitches.

Row 37: Chain 1 with white, tapestry crochet 34 white, 2 brown, 29 white stitches.

Rows 38 through 41: Chain 1 with white, then single crochet across with white, still carrying the beige and brown yarns.

Border

Round A: Single crochet a white border around the four sides, still carrying the beige and brown yarns.

Row B: Cut the beige and brown yarns flush. Repeat the following sequence with the white yarn, 33 times across the top: chain 8, single crochet 2 stitches. At the end of the row finish off, then work in the end.

Finishing

If part of the hanging is excessively wider or lumpy turn it over. From the back with a small crochet hook, pull some of the carried yarns until the hanging flattens out or narrows. The loops formed from pulling the carried yarns can be cut flush as long as they are secured on both sides.

Block the wall hanging. Insert the dowel in the loops at the top of the hanging.

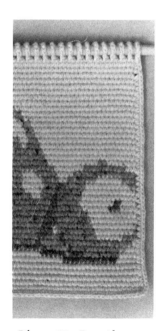

Photo 52. Detail showing border.

Suppliers List

For a complete list of textile suppliers, send $5 to:
Suppliers Directory
Handweavers Guild of America, Inc.
120 Mountain Avenue, B 101
Bloomfield, CT 06002.

A partial list of suppliers of mill end and other yarns used in the projects in this book follows. Write or call for current price lists.

Earth Guild
One Tingle Alley
Asheville, NC 28801
(800) 327-8448

Elite Yarns
12 Perkins Street
Lowell, MA 01854
(800) 343-0308

Frederick J. Fawcett, Inc. (linen)
1304 Scott Street
Petaluma, CA 94954
(800) 289-9276

The Fiber Studio
9 Foster Hill Road
P.O. Box 637
Henniker, NH 03242
(603) 428-7830

Linda Snow-Fibers
3209 Doctors Lake Drive
Orange Park, FL 32073

The Mannings
P.O. Box 687
East Berlin, PA 17316
(800) 233-7166

Patternworks (wide-handled crochet hooks, yarn)
P.O. Box 1690
Poughkeepsie, NY 12601
(914) 462-8000

R & M Yarn
Route 4, Martin Road
Cartersville, GA 30120
(404) 386-3413

Warp 'N Weave
2815 34th Street
Lubbock, TX 79410
(806)-799-0151

Wonder Craft/Bristol Yarn Corp.
1 Constitution Street
Bristol, RI 02809
(401) 253-2030

Yarn Barn
P.O. Box 1191
Canton, GA 30114
(404) 479-5083

Clock movements and accessories:
Check your local craft store, or contact:

Klockit
P.O. Box 636
Highway H North
Lake Geneva, WI 53147
(800) 556-2548

Plastic rods for hangings:
Almac Plastics, Inc.
47-42 37th Street
Long Island City, NY 11101
(800) 221-0710
Call to find the branch office in your area.

Wooden dowels can be purchased at local craft,
hardware and lumber stores.

Bibliography

Dittrick, Mark. *Hard Crochet.* New York: Hawthorn Books, Inc., 1978.

Feldman, Del Pitt. *Crochet Discovery and Design.* New York: Doubleday, 1972.

Halliday, Anne. *Decorating with Crochet.* Boston: Houghton Mifflin Co., 1975.

Mackenzie, Clinton. *New Design in Crochet.* New York: Van Nostrand Reinhold, 1972.

McCall's Knit/Crochet Encyclopedia. New York: McCall's Needlework and Craft Magazine, 1977.

Index

Supplement, pages 106-108: Three tapestry crochet graph papers for varying stitch heights.

Look for *Tapestry Crochet* and other DOS TEJEDORAS
titles at your favorite yarn shop or craft book store,
or write for a catalog to:

DOS TEJEDORAS
P. O. Box 14238
St. Paul, MN 55114

Andean Folk Knitting by Cynthia LeCount

Salish Indian Sweaters by Priscilla Gibson-Roberts

Latvian Mittens by Lizbeth Upitis

Creative Knitting by Mary Walker Phillips

Finishes in the Ethnic Tradition
by Baizerman and Searle

A Bevy of Embellishments by Beth Karjala

Rag Rug Handbook by Meany and Pfaff

An instructional Video for *Tapestry Crochet*
is available from:
Victorian Videos
P. O. Box 1540
Colfax, CA 95713